Be a Parent, Not a Pushover

*A Guide to Raising Happy,
Emotionally-Healthy Teens*

Maryann Rosenthal, Ph.D.
with Dale Fetherling

*Soledad Mountain Press
San Diego, California*

Be a Parent Not a Pushover

Copyright 2004 by Maryann Rosenthal

First U.S. edition 2004

Published in the United States by Soledad Mountain Press, San Diego, California
Distributed by Midpoint Trade Books, New York

Cover design and layout by Lorilee Art Services, San Diego, California
Interior design and layout by Robert Goodman, Silvercat™, San Diego, California

Publishers Cataloging in Print Data

Rosenthal, Maryann

Be a parent, not a pushover : a guide to raising happy, emotionally healthy teens / Maryann Rosenthal, with Dale Fetherling --1st ed. -- San Diego, Calif. : Soledad Mountain Press, 2004.

p. ; cm.
Includes bibliographic references and index.
ISBN 0-9740869-0-8

1. Parent and teenager. 2. Parenting. 3. Child psychology.4. Discipline. I. Fetherling, Dale. II. Title.

HQ799.15.R67 2004   2003092815
649/.125--dc22   0310

To my mother,

Grace Margaret Murphy,

who always encouraged me to
express and live my dreams
in spite of my fear.

Contents

# Acknowledgments

Writing this book has been a learning experience, a life experience, and a challenge, but most of all it has been a joy. It would never have been written had it not been for the unfailing support and expert knowledge of Dale Fetherling. Dale is a superb author and his constant support as a professional became a resource that I came to depend on throughout this journey. He helped me to turn a concept into substance. I can never thank him enough.

My husband, Joe, contributes to the richness of my life every day. His humor, devotion and love sustains me every step of the way. My deepest love for holding down the fort as my dream evolved.

The experience of guiding my children and stepchildren as they maneuver life has provided me with countless opportunities to make this book real. I am so proud of the adults they have become. They are the blessings of my life.

Dr. Denis Waitley has helped me to construct this stage of my professional life. I owe him such gratitude for his loving support as a friend. He is a natural genius for his original ideas and insights and he is a constant inspiration to me. I am honored to be his friend.

My warm and special thanks to my dear friend, Chris Taub for her editorial insight and ever-present red pen as we lay on the beach of Grand Cayman. To Patty Mack, a forever friend, for her helpful comments, support, and encouragement in writing this book.

My gratitude goes to Dr. Kent Layton who was never too busy to listen when difficulties would arise. He makes me laugh. Dr. Nancy Vader-McCormack gives true meaning to the word grace. She has taught me much about friendship and life. Dr. Kathryn Anderson is a dear friend whose support has sustained me throughout this journey. Dr. Richard Jordan is a gifted writer, colleague, and friend. He generated creative insights during difficult times. My appreciation goes to Joyce Churchill, who arrived in the eleventh hour to help with the final edit. I am so lovingly grateful to all of you.

I also want to thank my publicist, Antoinette Kuritz. She has been my guardian angel. Her support is unwavering and her creative energy is infectious and inspiring.

Shelly Nelson and Shelli Hutchison of Lorilee Art Services have captured the essence of the book visually. I am forever grateful for their creative cover design.

Bob Goodman, who patiently guided me to the completion of this journey. He calmed my fears constantly. Thank you.

Finally, I would like to thank all of the families and adolescents that are my clients. It is my privilege to work with them. They have provided the backbone for this book and without them, it could not have been written.

 # Foreword

*C*ongratulations! You have made a priceless investment in your family's future. If you are reading this, you care about children navigating the white-water rapids of the teen years and becoming healthy, happy, and well-adjusted young adults who can function effectively in a fast-forward global village where there are more changes in one day than in a decade of their parents' and grandparents' lives.

If you are reading this, you have—by choice or chance—discovered a truly remarkable and valuable guidebook providing strategies for success in eliminating the barriers between you and your teenage child or children.

This is *not* a "New Age" parenting treatment with the latest jargon and psychobabble on becoming your child's best friend and sidekick. It is *not* a compilation of articles and anecdotes offering overly simplistic answers or a false sense of security that "your kids are just going through a stage and will grow out of their irrational behavior." Many self-help books are published by clever writers and promoters who know how to sell fashionable ideas, without having direct experience in their subject. Refreshingly, this gem is a "fact" book, not a "fad" book, and is laser-accurate in its premise and in its promise.

Dr. Maryann Rosenthal is a consummate professional, author, and parent you can trust. Not only is she a friend and colleague of mine, but I have done my homework on her qualifications and counsel. She has first-hand experience and expertise, backed by breakthrough scientific research, to make the most difficult job in the world—*parenting*—easier, more productive and meaningful as well as more enjoyable.

Equally as important as her resume and track record as a highly regarded psychologist and therapist is her demonstrated leadership as a nurturing role model and mother for her own children. All are challenging themselves to realize their full potential in their own way and on their own terms.

In the pages that follow, Dr. Rosenthal first helps us understand the physiological and psychological turmoil associated with adolescence in today's society. She then gives us a mirror that helps us view and understand the reflection of our own parenting styles, whether authoritarian or authoritative, permissive or uninvolved. This is powerful, critically important work that teaches us how to love our teens while setting limits, how to be a coach, not merely a cheerleader.

Most of us parent by trial and error. We often repeat and perpetuate the mistake and prejudices of our parents. This book enables us to break that cycle by providing insights and practical action steps to help close the generation gap and solve the problems so prevalent in today's family life as adolescents attempt to gain the privileges of adults while maintaining the lack of accountability they feel entitled to as children.

Chicago Public Library

South Chicago
4/17/2015   3:40:10 PM
-Patron Receipt-

ITEMS BORROWED:

1:
Title: Be a parent, not a pushover : a guide
Item #: R0403658686
Due Date: 5/8/2015

-Please retain for your records-

Foreword

Dr. Rosenthal has wisdom, clarity, and real-life solutions to what's missing in our homes: *sustained, informed guidance by caring parents who can balance love with leadership.* This book would have been a godsend for me when I was raising my children, especially during the turbulent teens. I'm giving a copy to each of them before my grandchildren become teenagers.

Dr. Denis Waitley
Author of *Seeds of Greatness*
and *The Psychology of Winning*

Preface

You are not powerless to deal with your teenagers. But that power has to be wielded carefully, like a coach or a trainer, not a dictator or a drill sergeant. And you don't need to be a perfect parent, but you do need to hone certain skills and instincts.

Having worked in the field of human behavior for 15 years, I spend a great deal of time teaching adults to know the difference between their instincts and the brain chatter that gets in the way of true wisdom. In this book I hope to distill for you the essence of that knowledge and help you learn how to best use your power.

But, first, let me say that if you're motivated to pick up this book, I feel your pain. Your children are probably challenging you in ways that you could never have imagined. With their outrageous clothes and music, their frequent penchant for the bizarre, with wild mood swings, with their sporadic lack of respect for you, their indolence and even arrogance, they appear to taunt you. *We reject you,* they seem to cry out, *despite what you've done for us.*

Be a Parent, Not a Pushover

This is because teens are struggling to hold on to the joys of childhood even as they graduate into the threatening adult world. The very openness they exuded and were rewarded for as children seems to invite penalties as they grow beyond adolescence. A part of them wants to remain fun and free . . . and a part feels overwhelmed by the demands of growing up, of meeting your expectations, those of their peers, and those of the world at large. To make matters worse, their brains—and thus their ability to process information and make judgments—are changing.

The pendulum swings

So for them it's both an exciting and a scary time: They're exulting in their hoped-for independence even as they are frightened by the demanding, often-uncaring world of adulthood. Because they lack the experience to navigate in the adult world, their still-forming personalities often swing like a pendulum between two poles, such as:

> Shall we sulk? Or celebrate?
> Shall we become loners? Or crowd pleasers?

During this confusing period, they end up doing both and being both, often changing from one mode to the other so often and so rapidly that it confounds their parents. You probably find yourself asking, *Who is this person? And why is he or she so radically different than the son or daughter I knew last year, last week, or even yesterday?*

Eventually, these teens will figure out how to blend these disparate impulses and settle on a stance that works for them.

But because that cannot happen overnight, conflict is inevitable—within them, and between you and them. Parents are quick to blame this conflict on "raging hormones," but it's deeper and more delicate than that.

Not only do most parents misjudge the complexity of their teen's conflicts, but they also fail to understand their *own* paradoxes. Just as the kids struggle to find a balance between seizing life's joys and shielding themselves from its harshness, we parents wrestle continuously with finding the balance between loving our children and setting limits for them. Truly loving our children means recognizing that they need freedom but also discipline. When there's too much discipline, teens will rebel. When there's too much freedom, they hunger for structure and often find it in unsavory ways.

Finding that balance is not simple. It is what this book is about.

How this book is organized

I want to help parents to form a truly loving and satisfying relationship with their teens. To do so requires a parent to have self-knowledge as well as information about how their kids think and act.

Thus, the book is divided into three parts:

I. Understanding Teenage Turmoil
II. A-D-U-L-T: A Five-Step Plan for Eliminating Barriers Between You and Your Teen
III. Problem-Solving with Your Teen

Be a Parent, Not a Pushover

In the first part, we'll look at the physical and psychological changes your teen is going through and the ways in which your kid is looking for both love and leadership. We'll also turn our scrutiny inward to look at your parenting style and how that may affect your teen, especially when you get angry.

In addition to my academic training and experience as a therapist, I've learned about teens from raising them—four of my own and three stepchildren. Part II presents the core of what I've learned in the classroom, in my office, and in my home. I use the acronym ADULT (Awareness, Direction, Uniqueness, Love, and Teaching) to encompass the range of concepts that I believe a parent needs to master.

And finally, Part III gets very specific about how to problem-solve with your teen. Can you help them—*and yourself*—set and reach goals, shed stress, and develop strong character?

And at the end, I will try to sum up in an epilogue why time, love, and leadership are the only lasting riches you can share with your teen. Spend them wisely.

Storms of hurricane proportion

Being a parent is probably the most difficult and important job you or I will ever have. Adding to its difficulty is that most parents are haunted by their own insecurities and perhaps those of *their* parents. But that cycle can be broken.

At their best, the teen years are a choppy sea of feelings; at their worst, they bring emotional storms of hurricane proportions that create despair and sometimes disaster. But we must be positive and proactive. We can lessen—if not eliminate—these emotional storms if we care enough to learn. And we *can* learn if we care enough about our children.

Maryann Rosenthal, Ph.D.
La Jolla, California
September 2003

chapter 1

Why Does My Teen Act Like That?

Wasn't it only yesterday that Cindy, your 14 year old, would volunteer to do the laundry? Not only that, but she would then neatly fold the clothes from the dryer and put them away, singing softly to herself some gentle Beatles tune before asking if she could help with supper. She would prepare some avocado dip, greet your adult dinner guests warmly, then retire to her room to do her homework. You remember swelling with pride as your guests commented on what a polite, charming girl she was. "She's wonderful," you recall saying, "and I'm so lucky."

Well, maybe that wasn't yesterday, but it wasn't very long ago. But look at her now! Like some poster girl for grunge, she's wearing ratty clothes, spiky hair, and too much makeup. She's gotten her ears, nose, and tongue pierced. She listens only to the angry, indecipherable verse of some felon turned rap singer whose guttural utterances are played so loudly they rattle your internal organs. She sleeps a lot, and when awake, she closes her door and spends what seem like entire days in her room, watching TV or talking in muted, conspiracy-like tones to friends on the phone. Her grades have fallen. She's almost impossible to get up for school, and she refuses to do her chores. Her eyes look odd, and you worry that she might be smoking dope or drinking. Almost every day brings another unpleasant surprise in her speech or behavior.

You ask yourself: This is my child? What caused her to change like that? What did I do wrong? And how can we ever get back to where we were?

Problem behaviors

Most American kids navigate the critical transition years from 12 to 20 with relative success. Though they may be difficult at times, they don't grow up to be dope addicts or bank robbers or prostitutes. If there are decent schools, supportive families, and caring youth groups and churches, the kids evolve into reasonably well-adjusted participants in a technically advanced, democratic society. Even under less than optimal conditions, most become responsible, ethical adults.

But that certainly doesn't mean those years are easy, and "most" teens does not equal "all" teens. At least one quarter of all adolescents are at risk for engaging in dangerous behaviors that threaten their health and longevity.

Such problem behaviors among teens can have lots of causes. But behaviorists cite one of the most common: Lack of sustained guidance from caring adults. I would add: Lack of sustained guidance from informed, caring adults. The question for parents isn't just *do I care?* . . . but *how can I craft practical strategies for helping my teen maneuver along the path to successful adulthood?*

In this chapter we're going to look at some of a teen's needs, explore what could be some physical reasons for bad behavior, and try to provide some general, preliminary advice for beleaguered parents.

The big picture

On the whole, teenagers' relationships with their parents are far less stormy than what has been generally thought. Only a minority engages in open conflict or rebellion, though most teens seek in their own ways to establish their identity and autonomy. Through it all, most parents remain a positive influence on their teens.

Still, too many kids grow up without having their needs met. Then they yield to social pressures to use drugs, have sex, and engage in antisocial activities. Too many are alienated from school and may even drop out. Lots of examples exist, among rich and poor, of self-destructive, even violent, behavior.

But what kids are looking for is simple:

- Respect
- A sense of belonging to a valued group
- Useful skills, including social ones

While the needs are simple, achieving them is not. Ours is a complicated society, with lots of people and institutions—all of them flawed—influencing our teens. Those with the greatest influence in shaping kids are families, schools, youth-service organizations, and the media. All of these need strengthening.

Be a Parent, Not a Pubhover

The toughest job

And you—the parent—are potentially the biggest influence and have what's arguably the toughest job: To both give love and set limits. That's a theme we'll come back to many times in this book.

When teens fail to find respect, a sense of belonging, and useful skills, they often behave badly. Here's the voice of reality speaking English: Your actions and example will send powerful messages about what you expect from your children, *but that may not be enough to shape them exactly as you would like.* Peer pressure is another big influence (especially when parents are emotionally distant or neglectful), and teens have an intense need to respond to that peer audience.

Despite your best efforts, your teen probably will behave one way with you and another with his or her peers. For instance, probably most teenagers drink and even break the law on occasion. But that doesn't mean they're not wonderful kids and won't be responsible adults. My point is, cut them and yourself some slack: They don't need to be perfect, and they don't need to be just like you in order for them to turn into terrific adults and for you to be a successful parent.

But you *do* need to show both love and leadership. You've got to honor your children by encouraging them to grow toward independence. You've got to make it a point to enlist their opinions while still providing the structure within which those opinions operate. You've got to permit them to try to establish their own standards.

And above all, you've got to avoid childhood trauma—such as abuse, derision, and scorn . . . that causes your children to walk around in a permanent state of fear. Such hypervigilance will contribute to making them defensive and hostile for their entire lives. That's the way violent, remorseless children are created, and they, in turn, will create their own violent, remorseless offspring.

Males especially

Males especially need to know they can talk to you in safety. Boys, as Bill Pollack writes in *Real Boys*, may exhibit bravado but they find it more difficult to express their real selves even in private or with family and friends. We joke about how adult males won't ask for directions. But it's not so funny when many teenage males are reluctant to ask for directions of a larger kind, the moral kind, when they are lost.

Because the modern family doesn't allow enough time or energy for emotional nurturing to be given by mothers, Pollack says, boys are likely to imitate the worst characteristics of their fathers. Thus, they may deal with emotional needs through silence and withdrawal, through competitiveness, or through alcohol and anger. Boys raised like that may see partying as a way to hide their deepest feelings and to present a bold front to their peers.

But both girls and boys need to know there's one safe refuge—home. And one safe outlet for their feelings—talking to you.

The curse of wimpy parents

That *doesn't* mean their every need or want must be fulfilled, that the home must be like Burger King where "We do it *your* way." It *doesn't* mean bad behavior goes unnoted and unpunished. It *doesn't* mean teens ought to be exempted from work or responsibility. In fact, I think too many parents worry that their children will not like them and so they're constantly trying to curry favor. That's not the way a family, or any healthy relationship, ought to work.

In truth, as Judith Harris writes in *The Nurture Assumption*, parents are meant to be in charge. But too often they are reluctant to use that authority because of the advice given to them by experts: Be careful not to damage the child's self-esteem. And that's good advice as far as it goes, but the experience of previous generations shows that it is possible to raise well-adjusted children without having them believe the planets revolve around them alone.

In short, though this may sound harsh, *you should be a parent, not a pal.* You're not on earth just to fill their every waking hour with joy. You're a parent, not a cruise ship social director. The idea that parents should have to entertain their children would have been laughable to our ancestors.

You need to have an equal measure of steel and sympathy. We'll come back to the steel part later, but, meantime, let's look at one big factor that may encourage you to be a bit more sympathetic, or at least understanding, of how your teen functions.

Inside the teenage brain

The Columbine shootings in Colorado in 1999, followed by a spate of further school violence across the country, focused the nation's attention on aberrant teen behavior. Most teens, as I say, never come close to committing such violent acts. But that isn't to say their behavior—ranging from high-risk acts with cars and drugs to annoying mood swings—doesn't drive parents crazy. The bumper sticker *Insanity Is Heredity—We Get It From Our Kids* sets many adult heads nodding in agreement. But the point is there may be a physical basis for some of this adult-teen disconnect. Studies suggest that remarkable changes—much more than previously believed—occur in the brain during the teen years.

Emotions first

There's a lot that's not known about the brain, whether adult or teen. But more is being pieced together all the time. Until just a few years ago, for example, scientists believed that the brain was fully developed by the time a child reached the teen years. The implication was that a teenager *could* think like an adult if only he wanted to. But the 100 billion *neurons* (nerves) inside an adult skull, it turns out, aren't fully wired in most people until their early 20s. To complicate matters further, the different regions of the teenage brain develop on different schedules.

For instance—and this probably won't surprise any parent—the emotional centers of the teenage brain are up and running well before those that help the teen make sound decisions and keep emotions in check. This may go far toward explaining why an otherwise sane 17-year-old may go a little nuts when faced with a "mosh pit" at an all-night dance, or why he can be praising you one moment and saying he hates you the next.

Be a Parent, Not a Pushover

That leads us to the issue of teenage moodiness and all-around irritability. According to the accepted wisdom, teens rebel against their parents and all authority figures as they seek to define who they are and to stake out their independence. Many a movie (starting with James Dean in *Rebel without a Cause*) has revolved around the young iconoclast, a character type who's become as familiar to us as the cowboy loner or the slightly unscrupulous private eye. Another rationale for teen irascibility has been the all-purpose one of "hormones." Along with sexual stirrings and pimples, bad behavior was said to be caused by some chemical floodgate being lifted, allowing the dreaded hormones to wash away reason and decorum.

But more recent research suggests it's at least partly the brain that makes teens act weirdly. Scientists for some time have been studying the brain's structure. But now neuroscientists using functional MRI (magnetic resonance imaging) are able to measure how the brain performs tasks.

A work in progress

What they have found is that while 95% of the human brain has developed by the age of six, the greatest spurts of growth after infancy occur just around adolescence. So teen brains are still a work in progress. Thus, when you don't see eye to eye with your teen, you might want to take a moment to reflect on the possibility that part of the problem may be physical, not just attitudinal. But consider also how this three-pound mass of still-changing matter holds a universe of potential, too.

For instance, Dr. Jay Giedd of the National Institute of Mental Health looked at the brains of 145 normal children by scanning them at two-year intervals. This allowed Giedd and his team to chart for the first time normal brain development from childhood through adolescence. What they were surprised to find was that an area of the brain known as the prefrontal cortex appears to be growing again just before puberty. Although it was known that the brain of a baby grew by over-producing synapses (connections between brain cells) and then consolidating by pruning them back, it wasn't known that there was this second period of overproduction.

Another part of the brain that seems to change well into adolescence is the cerebellum. In fact, it may not finish growing until a person is well into his or her early 20s. Once thought to just be involved in muscle coordination, the cerebellum now is believed to help coordinate our thinking processes, too.

Giedd believes that the brain's second spurt of growth and pruning is particularly important. What teens do or do not do during this period could affect them for the rest of their lives. In effect, they may be hardwiring their brain to do sports, music, mathematics, or video games. He calls this "the use it or lose it" principle and suggests that how teens spend their time could become crucial as to what skills and interests they'll eventually have. Of course, there's a lot that isn't known about how these capacities may be influenced by other factors, such as teachers, society, nutrition, genes, or even bacterial or viral infections.

Be a Parent, Not a Pushover

Brain research

Let's take a simplified look at some other brain research and what light it may shed on teen behavior. Then we'll try to distill what this might mean for parents.

Flawed judgment and risk-taking

This is a common parental complaint. But blame it on the part of the brain that processes emotions and makes decisions. As I mentioned, the teen's prefrontal cortex, where judgments are formed, is slow to develop while his or her limbic system, where anger and other raw emotions are born, goes full-speed ahead. The limbic system, deep in the middle of the brain, is associated with gut reactions, sparking instant waves of fear, say, at the sight of a snarling tiger, or unbridled joy at a last-minute, winning shot in basketball.

Adults have such emotions, too, of course. But the adult's prefrontal cortex, which keeps tabs on the other parts of the brain, is more developed and keeps the limbic system in check. Indeed, the brain works almost like a team, with the prefrontal cortex being akin to a coach who oversees the carrying out of the team's various tasks. But in the case of teens, the "coach" (prefrontal contex) is not yet on the field, and the "players" (limbic system) are running amok.

Other research has shown that levels of serotonin, a chemical that helps transmit electrical signals between neurons, appears to decline temporarily in many adolescents. This also could encourage impulsive behavior.

Thus, the teen, lacking the "hardware" and perhaps the chemistry, too, for making good judgments, may tend to leap before looking. This tendency comes at a time in life when it's natural to seek out new experiences, including some risky ones. The two tendencies—a willingness to try almost anything and to not think clearly about the consequences— are a scary combination.

Getting a tattoo, driving too fast, smoking, drinking, shoplifting and other relatively low-level but potentially dangerous thrills may be signs of this risk-taking bent. Be aware, though, that some research suggests that about 60 percent of a teenager's tendency to act impulsively and misjudge potential danger is genetic. Are you a risk-taker, too?

Poor organizational skills

In a celebrated test at a Massachusetts hospital, adults and teenagers viewed photographs of people's faces contorted in fear. Asked to identify the emotion being expressed, every adult subject got it right. But only about half the teens could correctly identify the emotion as fear.

What's the implication? That you may be wrong if you assume you and the teen understand the same things in the same way. This and other research suggests that teens may differ from adults in what's coming into their brains, how it's being organized, and how they then respond to it. Thus, it may be unfair to expect teens to have adult-like organizational or decision-making skills before their brains are done growing.

For instance, let's say you give your teen a list of chores that need to be done before she can go to the movies. And a half hour later, almost nothing has been done. You may think she's being confrontational, doubting your resolve and challenging your authority.

But the truth may be that she heard the information but it just didn't register, or she heard but thought she could do it later. Or something else happened—maybe a friend came by or something good came on TV—that rearranged her priorities. That's not intended as an excuse for laziness, but rather to suggest that if teens can't as easily keep track of multiple thoughts and tasks, you may want to temper justice with mercy.

One of the last steps in making a teenage brain into an adult brain is the coating of nerves in white matter, known as myelin. This allows electrical impulses to travel down a nerve faster and more efficiently. Researchers now believe some myelinating continues until our early 20s.

Some of the nerves that become sheathed late connect areas of the brain that regulate emotion, judgment, and impulse control. Some nerves myelinate in girls earlier than in boys, which may help explain why teenage girls seem more emotionally mature than boys.

Aggressiveness and irritability

In both sexes, surges of testosterone at puberty swell the amygdala, an almond-shaped part of the limbic system that generates feelings of fear and anger. This effect is especially pronounced in boys, but it may account for the rise in aggressiveness and irritability seen in both sexes at adolescence.

Anorexia

Once thought to be entirely the result of cultural pressures on girls to be thin, anorexia and bulimia are now believed to be related also to changes in the brain. Girls with eating disorders have higher than average levels of serotonin.

People with high levels of serotonin can be obsessive and anxious. Some scientists now believe that while the need to be "perfect" may start a girl down the anorexic path, what keeps them going is that not eating makes them feel better. That's because food contains a component of a protein that's necessary for the body to produce serotonin. Thus, by starving themselves, girls may ease their anxiety by lowering the amount of serotonin in their brains.

Sleeping too much

For years, it's been assumed teens went to bed at increasingly later times because of their more active social lives or school pressures or perhaps just because they're trying to exercise their independence. But scientists now believe a major reason may be due to changes in the brain's biological timing system that governs sleep and wakefulness.

What we call the biological clock is actually the neurons in the brains that send signals to every part of the body. They control virtually all of the body's internal processes and their timing, including sleep.

Older adolescents are likely to be unable to fall asleep as early as they did when they were a few years younger. As a result, they should be sleeping later if they're to awaken rested. Yet despite this scientific fact, nearly all schools in the country have senior high schoolers going first, which means sending them to school in the last third of the sleep period. Researchers still don't know why this delay occurs or what causes the sleep cycle to shift back to a more normal schedule in adulthood.

Lessons Learned

For sure, it's clear that adolescence is a busy time for the brain and that the teen brain is a good deal more complicated than was once thought. The evidence suggests that teenagers literally think differently than adults.

So maturity is not simply a matter of slipping "software" (learning) into existing equipment. Instead the "hardware" (brain) itself is changing. And this has profound implications for understanding teen thinking and behavior. But other than recognizing that some of the difficulties with your teen may stem from changes in his or her brain, what can you do?

Some ideas:

Give them plenty of new experiences

While searching for new experiences is a normal part of growing up, you can help by providing healthy sources of stimulation. For one kid, being in the school play or volunteering in the community may provide plenty of excitement. For another, it could take hang-gliding lessons. The problem, of course, is that safe risks are not always available to the kids who need them. Middle-class kids can go snorkeling or water-skiing, but for many kids, there's just crime, sex, and drugs unless parents step in with alternative activities.

During adolescence, many higher mental skills will become automatic. Kids who exercise their brains, in effect, by learning to marshal their thoughts, to measure their impulses, and to understand abstract concepts, may be laying the neural foundations that will serve them for the rest of their lives.

If so, that argues for encouraging your teenager to hardwire his or her brain for good purposes. Do you want to hardwire it for reading, playing music, and doing mathematics—or for watching *Jerry Springer* on TV? This hard-wiring also provides yet another reason for teens not to take drugs or alcohol, because they may permanently alter the balance of chemicals in their brains.

While you don't want to dictate their passions, there's a lot you can do to stimulate their interest in life's joys. Keep good books around and talk about what you learned from them. Make music and musical training available. Travel and offer to take them along. Sample the world of nature through activities like hikes, gardening, and films. Keep physically active and encourage lifetime sports. Go to theaters, museums, concerts. Talk about these experiences . . . but don't be controlling: Let them draw their own conclusions.

Cut them some slack on their sleeping habits

They're not necessarily being lazy but instead are resetting chemicals in their emotional centers. If they get up too soon, they miss out on the phase of sleep that boosts memory and learning. Schools—and much of civilized life—start earlier than your kid's circadian clock.

Be a Parent, Not a Pushover

But what you can do is emphasize sleep's importance and try to help your teenager more through biology. For example, to encourage him or her to go to bed at a decent hour, keep lights low in the evening and open the curtains in the morning. Light absorbed through the eyes can reset their clock. And discourage them from going to bed in the wee hours on the weekend and snoozing until noon. That only disrupts the brain's clock. On weekends, try to get them to go to bed within an hour or two of their usual bedtime, then sleep in an hour or two the following morning.

Oppose the levels of violence and decadence that our kids are exposed to

Make your voice heard that gratuitous sex and violence are not acceptable. (See Chapter 4 for specific alternatives.)

Listen to your teen

You talk to your teen, but do you *listen*, do you really hear? Read and follow the good-listening practices in Chapter 3.

Remember the wisdom of your grandmother

Adolescence is fascinating and complex and fascinatingly complex in any one's life span. The physical and psychological changes the teen is going through are the most profound he/she will ever face in such a short period.

My strong suspicion is that the more advanced the science of the brain becomes, the more it will lead back to some very basic tenets of spending loving, quality time with our kids when their brains and their personalities are just forming.

Science may be leading us to the bedrock truth of what our grandmothers could have told us: *A parent needs to spend a lot of time with their kids.* Much of the rest of this book will detail how that can best be done.

chapter 2

Parent, Know Thyself

*T*here's nothing like living with a teenager to make you examine yourself and your values. Everywhere you turn, it's as if you're looking in a mirror. If you are angry, your child likely will have anger. If you are overly strict, your kid may rebel. If you're overly permissive, your child can become spoiled. Every action has a reaction.

Those do's and don'ts mount up until you may feel that when you look at your teen, that "mirror" is like the ones in the funhouse, with images wildly distorted from what you know them to be. So it's important to try to think clearly about how you come across to your kids. Thus, in this chapter, we will take a look at parenting styles and how those may affect your teen, especially when you get angry.

But here's the bottom line: Teens navigate life's maze by using two "stars," two guideposts: one is you, and one is their friends and associates. While the teens probably don't recognize it as such, their world is split roughly in half: parents and peers. Or at least it's theoretically split evenly. Depending on your actions, your part of that sphere of influence can grow or shrink . . . and the peer portion can expand or decrease proportionately.

It's the relationship, the tension, the gravitational pull between those two forces that colors so much of the teens' lives, that defines how they will respond to challenges and temptations. Thus, the more influence you have, the less the peers will have. And probably vice versa.

We're going to look at the world of the peer group in Chapter 10. But, first, let's hold the mirror up to yourself and your degree of influence: How do you parent? And how do you handle anger?

A matter of styles

You probably fret a lot about individual child-rearing decisions. After all, even before a child is born, you need to make critical choices: breastfeed or bottle, home care vs. nanny care, continue to work vs. staying home. And as the child gets older, the number of crucial decisions seem to grow: Should your 10-year-old be allowed to watch TV before he does his homework? Can a 14-year-old go to a dance without a chaperon? Is your 16-year-old responsible enough to handle a car? How much freedom should be given to a 17-year-old in choosing a college or a vocation or, for that matter, even a potential mate?

These are all important, day-to-day decisions. But in the long run what counts for more is your overall style, your broad pattern of parenting. Most kids will be able to handle a big decision or two that goes against them if they are comfortable with the overall relationship between you and them. It's important that this relationship, though it's generally unspoken, be clear and consistent. I believe it's that overall style or pattern of action—rather than a specific decision—that will most affect a teen's behavior. Generally, psychologists have found that there are two main components of parenting styles. One is responsiveness, or how much independence you're willing to grant. The other, for lack of a better word, is demandingness, how much strict obedience you require. How much obedience parents demand, how much freedom they grant, and how these two behaviors mesh go a long way toward defining the parents' style.

These parenting styles fall into four broad categories. Though different researchers give different names to them, the styles usually are said to be:

Authoritarian

Authoritarian parents are very strict and controlling. They have a strong sense of justice and of the need for obedience. They're big believers in clearly stated rules. If their kids don't "see the light" (behave as ordered), then those teens will "feel the heat" (be punished.) Such parents take a dim view of being challenged. Give-and-take with their children is discouraged. Thus, these parents are highly demanding but not very responsive.

Researchers believe children of authoritarian parents tend to be timid, have lower self-esteem, lack spontaneity, and rely to an unusual degree on the voice of authority.

Be a Parent, Not a Pushover

Authoritative

While retaining authority and control, these parents are warmer and more communicative than Authoritarian parents. Authoritative parents seek a balance between the teens' desire for independence and the parents' desire to be listened to.

These parents are demanding and responsive. They're assertive but not intrusive or restrictive. They want their children to be assertive as well as socially responsible and self-regulated as well as cooperative.

The best-adjusted children, researchers have found, often have parents with an Authoritative style. Both the Authoritarian and the Authoritative parents have high expectations for their children, but the Authoritative parent encourages more freedom of expression. So the child more likely develops a sense of independence. Such kids tend to develop into more competent adults than children brought up in the other styles.

Permissive

Permissive parents, while often warm and accepting, make few demands on their children. They're lenient, avoid confrontation, and allow considerable self-regulation. They may worry about thwarting the child's creativity and sense of self. They're much more responsive than they are demanding.

Sometimes the Permissive style is based on confusion. The parents are so out of touch with the adolescent world that the best they can do is to try to be a pal to the teen. So they tend to give adolescents what they ask for. Unfortunately, a lot of parents fall into this category.

Other Permissive parents want to compensate for what they themselves lacked as children. Perhaps they grew up in poverty and/or had parents who were overly strict. So as a result, seeing themselves as an ally to their teen, these parents bend over backwards to give the teen both the freedom and the material goods they lacked.

Yet other Permissive parents act conditionally. They view the teen as a mini-adult and give him or her what he or she wants, provided the teen satisfies certain parental demands. Making good grades, for example, may be linked to freedom and material benefits.

Or, at its most lax, permissiveness may take the form of indifference. The parents are just too busy, poor, troubled, or self-involved to exert much control. They may give material goods and freedom in return for the teen's implicit promise not to demand much from the parent.

Uninvolved

The uninvolved parent demands almost nothing and gives almost nothing in return, except near-absolute freedom. This style is low in both demandingness and responsiveness. At its worst, it can verge into neglect.

In practice

How would these parenting styles work in practice? For example, a teen wants to go with a bunch of friends on a weekend outing to Mexico where, the parent suspects, wild partying is on the agenda because of younger drinking-age requirements there.

Be a Parent, Not a Pushover

An Authoritarian parent might say: *No way! And if I ever catch you going down there without my permission, you'll be in big trouble. Don't even think about it.*

An Authoritative parent may respond: *No, I don't want you to go down there right now with your friends. I want to check it out with some other parents. If it looks O.K., maybe you can go later with your buddies.*

A Permissive parent would say: *Sure, go and have fun, but be careful.*

An Uninvolved parent may reply: *Whatever!*

Parenting style has been found to predict children's well-being in a number of areas, including social skills, academic performance, and the degree of problem behavior. The Authoritarian, Permissive, and Uninvolved styles can carry a high cost.

Children of Authoritarian parents, for example, may do well in school and not engage in problem behavior, but they tend to have poorer social skills, lower self-esteem, and higher levels of depression. They may grow up to be highly anxious people who don't realize their full potential because, figuratively speaking, they're always looking over their shoulder for that overly-demanding parent.

The teens of Permissive parents may come to feel entitled to privileges and material goods. If the parents try to regain control, the teen probably will perceive that effort to be a power struggle. He or she may fight back in dangerous ways, including sexual rebellion, unsavory associates, or substance abuse. Thus, they're more likely to be involved in problem behavior and perform less well in school, though they have higher self-esteem, better social skills, and lower levels of depression than Authoritarian children.

And Uninvolved parents, of course, can sow a lifetime of havoc by their indifference or inability to deal with their teen.

Authoritative parenting, which balances clear, high parental demands with emotional responsiveness and recognition of the child's need for autonomy, is one of the most consistent predictors of social competence. Thus, the child of Authoritative parents typically does well in school, develops good social skills, and avoids problem behaviors.

Studies show that the benefits of Authoritative parenting and the disadvantages of Uninvolved parenting are evident as early as the preschool years and continue throughout adolescence and into early adulthood. A recent study of 1,000 teens, for instance, by the National Center on Addiction and Substance Abuse (CASA) evaluated a "hands-on" (roughly equivalent to the Authoritarian or Authoritative styles) approach versus a "hands-off" (akin to the Permissive or Uninvolved styles) approach to parenting and found that teens living with "hands-on" parents are at only 25% of the risk for drug abuse than those living in "hands-off" households.

Similarly, 47% of teens in "hands-on" households reported having an excellent relationship with their fathers and 57% an excellent relationship with their mothers. By contrast, 13% of teens with "hands-off" parents reported an excellent relationship with their fathers and 24% with their mothers.

"Moms and dads should be parents to their children, not pals," said Joseph Califano Jr., former U.S. Secretary of Health, Education and Welfare (and president of CASA) in summing up the study. "Mothers and fathers who are parents rather than pals can greatly reduce the risk of their children smoking, drinking, and using drugs."

Which style are you?

Probably every parent uses some combination of these styles, depending on the issue and their own experiences. But in most cases, one style predominates. So you might want to do some thinking about your style as suggested in *A Parenting Style Assessment* box on page 27.

Negotiating about style

The good news is that most parents and teenagers have a basic reservoir of caring for one another and that can help you over the rough spots. Most teens can acknowledge that there are legitimate areas of their lives over which their parents can and should exercise control. And most parents want their kids to have enough freedom to develop into emotionally healthy, self-reliant individuals. But if there are any "no" or "sort of" answers to questions 5–8, you may need to do some foundational work.

Here's what I suggest. In one of your calmer moments, sit down with your teen and talk as frankly as you can about why you make the rules and decisions that you do. If need be, explain how you were raised and why the rules that your parents created did or didn't work in your life. State your love for your teen, of course, but also the reasons for your decisions. Don't just arbitrarily set boundaries because "that's the way it is" or because "I'm the grownup and you're the kid."

A Parenting Style Assessment

1. On a scale of 1–10 (with 10 being most demanding of obedience), how do you compare to:

    Other parents you know? __
    Your own parents? __
    Your spouse? ____

2. On a scale of 1–10 (with 10 being the most freedom-granting), how do you compare to:

    Other parents you know? __
    Your own parents? __
    Your spouse? __

3. Thus, you conclude your predominate parenting style is:

    Authoritarian __   Authoritative __
    Permissive __   Uninvolved __

4. List three recent situations in which your interaction with your teen revealed your parenting style:

    a.
    b.
    c.

5. Reviewing those three situations, does your style appear to be consistent over time?

    Yes___ No ____Sort of ____

6. If you have more than one child, is your style consistent from child to child?

Yes___ No ____Sort of ____

7. Have you explained to your teen/teens how and why your parenting style has evolved?

Yes___ No ____Sort of ____

8. Does your teen accept your style?

Yes___ No ____Sort of ____

Talk with your teen about what those areas are and the extent of your desired influence. Get their response. How much control do they believe they should have? How much freedom do they want or feel they need? Where are the sticking points?

If this sounds like negotiation, that's because it is. And that's how adults and soon-to-be adults should chart their differences and come up with workable solutions. In fact, not only should you discuss the present situation but also how power will be divided in the future. What you'll want to aim for is the gradual extension of authority to the teen.

In this way, the teen will develop decision-making skills while still under your protection.

The role of anger

No matter what your parenting style, you can sabotage it—and your relationship with your youngster—by how you act when you get angry. Sure, it's easy to become angered. Your teen purposely disobeys . . . or doesn't think about the consequences of what he or she is doing . . . or is rude and disrespectful . . . or, well, the possibilities are endless and inevitable.

But what's not inevitable is how you respond when irritating behavior occurs. You can easily cause more anger in you and in your teen depending on how you react.

For instance, Jamie, 17, is an excellent student, a talented athlete, and an overall good kid. He's the oldest of four children, and I had been working with his mom, Laurie, in therapy for quite some time.

But one day she seemed unusually frustrated. Her voice was quivering. "What bothered me most," she said, "was my lack of control." Jamie for weeks had been exhibiting increasing bouts of anger and animosity, most of it directed at his younger brother. On this particular day, Jamie had promised his brother and his friends that he would drive them to the beach. They've always done things together, so that seemed perfectly normal.

At the very last minute, though, Jamie refused, saying, "I'm not taking the little jerk. He and his idiot friends can get another ride."

"Jamie, you agreed, and I've made other plans, so please keep your word," his mother reasoned. "You've been planning this all week long."

Be a Parent, Not a Pushover

"What is it you want from me? He's a creep. I hate him, and I'm not going," Jamie countered.

Jamie and his mom continued to argue with one another, accomplishing nothing. The arguing soon turned to screaming.

"I'm not good at this," Laurie told me softly.

"Not good at what?" I asked.

"I felt myself getting all worked up, and I knew I was losing control. It was awful . . . ." She couldn't finish and started to cry.

Finally, Laurie insisted that both she and Jamie sit down and say absolutely nothing until they had both cooled down. Later, when Jamie's dad came home, they all were able to sit down and get to the heart of the matter. It turned out Jamie's outgoing younger brother seemed to be overshadowing him at school and at home. Jamie was older, but he was shy and lacked confidence. He watched as his brother "got the cute girls" and, generally, just had more fun. So Jamie was angry and needed to vent. But Laurie felt guilty for losing control.

"Laurie," I told her, "You're only human, and you're not perfect. But you did the right thing by calling the 'time out' and halting the escalating anger. You stopped the battle. Good for you!"

We spent some time exploring the ways in which Laurie manages and handles her anger, and I supported her efforts not to let disagreements soar out of hand. In the weeks that followed, Laurie reported that things got much better since that day. In fact, she later said, "Things are better than they've been for a long time. It's as if a heavy weight has been lifted from our household."

Parents need to deal with their own anger, too. There are three important questions you need to be able to answer if you are to handle your own anger:

- When is it valid?
- When is it needless?
- When does it become a problem?

When is it valid? It's always valid. Anger is an emotion, a feeling. When your son's inattentiveness results in a crumpling of the fender of the family car, you have a right to feel anger. Acknowledge that. Rather than feeling guilty about being angry, you should acknowledge that anger is occurring, then try to get to the bottom of it, which leads to the second question.

When is it needless? Anger is needless when it doesn't do any good and it makes matters worse by upsetting you, your teen, and those around you, too. If you yell and scream at your son that's he "an idiot" for denting the car, does that make the fender whole? No. Does it make him a better driver? No. Does it help improve this situation? Definitely not. Does it worsen the whole situation. You bet!

If it doesn't help, it's needless anger. But anger often becomes needless because of the way you use it. If you think clearly and act accordingly, you may be able to transform needless anger into what's called adaptive anger. Name-calling and cursing about the dented fender is needless. But if you can use your anger to finally get motivated to get the kid long-delayed driving lessons, that's something else. Or to talk to him about the high cost of car insurance and how he needs to contribute to paying the increase that will be levied because of this mishap. Anger, thus, can be a source of energy.

Becoming more familiar with both the positive and negative functions of anger will help you know when your anger is needless. What's positive about anger? Well, for one thing, it energizes you. The body girds for self-defense. Blood pressure rises, adrenaline flows, breathing becomes more rapid, stamina grows, and in general, the body prepares for a fight. That doesn't mean you have to fight. Rather, it means you're stronger, more physically capable.

Second, anger is a release. It's a way of venting tension and communicating our negative feelings to others. How we do that communicating is the key.

Third, anger imparts information about people and situations. It yields a clue that there's something worrisome or threatening going on. It signals to us a problem that needs to be dealt with.

But on the flip side, anger has lots of negatives. It can confuse our thinking and cause us to act impulsively, without considering the consequences. It can put us in a defensive posture in which we seek to protect our pride at all costs. Perhaps most importantly, anger can prompt aggression as we try to take it out on something or someone.

You can seek to reduce needless anger by minimizing anger's negative function and using its positive ones. When you feel yourself getting angry, ask yourself:

Your Relationship with Anger

Are you aware of your anger? Of your teen's anger? You may be frightened by expressions of anger in either of you. Perhaps one or both of you are bottling it up and are afraid of letting it out. Or perhaps you express it in counterproductive ways.

Completing the following sentences will help your explore your relationship with anger and with your teen's anger:

1. When I get angry, I feel

2. I usually express my anger by

3. When my teen gets angry, I

4. I try to avoid getting angry by

5. My teen usually expresses anger by

6. When my teen gets angry, I

7. When I am angry, my teen sees me as

8. When my teen is angry, I see him/her as

Am I using my anger as a release and a source of energy to defend myself against being abused or treated unfairly? Am I finding out important information about a problem I need to deal with? If so, that's adaptive.

Or,

Am I letting the anger distort my thinking and make me act impulsively, maybe even with physical or verbal aggression against someone who didn't mean to hurt me? If so, that's needless.

Anger is adaptive when it helps you, needless when it hurts you or others. In the case of the dented car fender, for example, if you react aggressively, you'll probably make a bad, minor situation into a bad, major situation. You won't find out what really happened, how the kid really feels, and you won't be able to explore ways to avoid a repetition.

In situations you can't change, use your anger to prevent them from recurring. Anger may always be ugly, but it doesn't have to be bad. Learning to use its positive qualities will actually help you.

When anger becomes a problem

Even the most calm among us experiences needless anger at some point. Don't beat yourself up for that. But do be alert to whether it happens too often. Try to make a distinction between the times when anger is useful and when it's harmful.

It's harmful when it happens too often. It's harmful when it's too severe, too intense and wildly disproportionate to the cause. It's harmful when it lasts too long; a long-lasting anger keeps the body in an abnormal state and, more important, may get in the way of a resolution of the conflict. Anger is harmful when it interferes with your doing a good job or being generally liked by people. And, of course, it's harmful when it leads to aggression. Both verbal aggression, such as calling someone a name, or physical aggression are signs that your anger has become a major problem.

Be a Parent, Not a Pushover

If it's any or all of these, you probably need to seek professional help, such as a therapist. Your anger threatens to ruin your relationship with your teen and probably with others as well.

Ways of dealing with anger

But even if your anger is not a "problem," you ought to be aware of how you deal with it. There are three basic kinds or styles of anger management. Usually we learn to use one of these styles as youngsters by the way our parents dealt with anger or the way they handle ours. (See sidebar, "Anger Messages I Was Taught . . . and Teach.")

Stuffing is when you avoid the person or situation that is provoking the anger and "stuff" it inside by denying it exists. But, of course, it does exist; you are just hiding it. Maybe you hide it because your parents made it clear that expressing anger was a no-no. Or maybe you fear hurting the other person, or you fear rejection, or aren't confident you'll be able to deal with the emotional upset of a conflict. So you walk away even when you're boiling inside.

Stuffing is not a good anger-management style because, for one thing, stuffed anger is inevitably expressed in some other form. It might be migraine headaches, ulcers, depression, sleeplessness, or obesity, but it's expressed nonetheless.

Secondly, whatever provoked your anger is unchanged. You haven't confronted the person or the issue. So the provocation continues as does the stuffing and its harmful effects.

Denying you are angry and withdrawing is not compatible with a good relationship with your teen (or anyone else.)

Anger Messages I Was Taught . . . and Teach

As children and young adults, we all learned ways of dealing with anger. It's sometimes helpful to review those implied messages as a way of understanding the anger-dealing habits we've adapted. Try assessing the messages about anger you were taught by the following:

Mother:

Father:

Siblings:

Teachers:

You, in turn, as a parent send implied messages to your teen about how to handle anger. How would you describe the message you send?

If you wish to change that message, what would the new message be?

What actions can you take to make sure that new message gets across?

1.

2.

3.

You don't take the opportunity to work out the problem. Instead, tension rises until, eventually, there is an explosion. Then you hear: "Why didn't you tell me this before?"

Escalating is another way of handling anger, and it's at least equally bad. The "escalator" gives free rein to the instinctive fight response by returning fire. Each purported attack is countered with an equal or more vicious response: "You think I'm a nincompoop? Well, you're a ___." Or you ask accusatory questions: "How do you dare think that?" or "Who gave you a right to say that?" Or you blame: "It's all your fault, you

____!" Or try to shame: "How could you say that to me after all that I've done for you? You're selfish and spoiled."

Again, this is a counterproductive style because through your ranting and raving, you're seeking to control the situation by making things worse. The result: Nothing gets solved. Even if your opponent is intimidated into backing off temporarily, the problem is heightened, and you can literally kill yourself with a heart attack if you do this a lot.

Constant escalating is a terrible habit that destroys relationships and often brings violence with it.

Directing is a more productive anger style. A director tells his opponent clearly and appropriately why he is angered. He makes eye contact, keeps his voice level in check, and says something like, "I am angry because you deceived me" or "I want you to tell me the whole truth."

People who express anger directly get their message across without belittling the other person, without bottling up the anger inside of themselves, and without, in effect, throwing gasoline on the flames. They don't call their antagonist a nasty name, and they don't try to accuse, shame, or blame. Instead, they state how the other person's words or actions affect them. ("When you do that, I feel like____." Or, "It makes me ____ when you say those things. Can you understand why I would feel that way?")

Being a director isn't easy, especially if you grew up in a household of stuffers or escalators. But it's a powerful technique and worth practicing.

Directing your anger, however, isn't a panacea. Your teen may slough off your attempts at anger management by either ignoring your message or by getting defensive. This can lead to frustration, further anger of your own, and, at worse, escalation.

Let's say you try to talk to him about the dented fender:

"Son, we need to talk about that trouble with the car."

Whatever, he says blankly, looking away or walking from the room.

Or worse, he responds defiantly, *Sue me. I don't care.*

Or worse yet, *What a joke! You're the world's worst driver. And you taught me to drive—if you can call that "teaching"—so how can you be such a hypocrite and criticize me when you're such a complete idiot behind the wheel? Everybody thinks so. Even my friends laugh at the totally dumb way you drive.* [He may throw in a swear word or two, just to try to rattle you.]

He's playing defense, trying to knock you off balance and block your attempt at communication. That's what some people do to avoid confronting anger or dealing with distress. How do you respond?

Well, your job just got harder, but you need to stick with your plan of directing your anger, not stuffing or escalating it. Don't yield to the temptation to reply in kind.

Here's how you might reply to keep the dialogue on track.

Him: *Whatever.*

You: "The 'whatever' is that there's several hundred dollars damage to the car. Perhaps you and I both need to improve our driving, and we can talk about that. But, in any event, we need to figure out how to prevent this from happening again."

If he walks away, follow him. If he won't talk now, promise him you'll talk later—and do so.

Him: *Sue me, I don't care.*

You: "I think you do care. You're a good kid, and this is not the end of the world. But we need to come up with a plan for how to avoid this kind of thing in the future. Work with me on this."

Him: *What a joke! You're the world's worst driver. And you taught me to drive—if you can call that "teaching"—so how can you be such a hypocrite and criticize me when you're such a complete idiot behind the wheel? Everybody thinks so. Even my friends laugh at the totally dumb way you drive.*

You: "Well, you've got a point there. But the more pressing point is the car outside with the banged-up fender, which you were driving at the time. How are we going to keep this from happening again?"

All three of your responses are based on the same tactic: You overcome defensiveness by not becoming defensive yourself. When you communicate non-defensively, you persist in a non-hostile way, and you limit the physical expression of anger. That makes it easier to come up with alternative ways of getting your message across.

Be a Parent, Not a Pushover

Lessons Learned

"If you want things to be different," said Dr. Norman Vincent Peale, "perhaps the answer is to become different yourself."

What is your parenting style? How do your rate in responsiveness vs. demandingness? Should you be trying to change your style? In what ways?

Is your mode of anger expression sabotaging your style? In the real world and in real life, we all get angry. Don't be too critical of yourself for that. But do try to channel it in the most useful ways. Failure to do so just creates more anger in you and in your teen.

After all, you're supposed to be the mature one. So show it by taking really strong steps toward directing, not stuffing or escalating it.

Here's a short course on what to do the next time you feel a stab of anger:

Step 1: Breathe. (Focus on your breath if only for a moment or two. That'll help calm you.)

Step 2: Relax. (Try to take a longer view. Whatever your teen has done or said won't account for much over the long term.)

Step 3: Ask yourself what you're trying to accomplish. (Is it to immediately resolve the issue? It probably shouldn't be. Instead, what you should be aiming for is a dialogue with your teen that will lead to a more appropriate response to such situations in the future.)

Step 4: Aim away. (Don't counterpunch and escalate the argument. Focus on keeping the conversation going but directing it toward a solution devoid of blame or shame or name-calling.)

Step 5: Persist. (Don't let the teen's defensiveness sidetrack your effort to move toward a workable solution.)

Step 6: Keep focused on the future. (Don't belabor the past or fret about the present. Imagine the relationship you would like to have with your teen a year from now, in five years, or even in 10 years. That's what you're working toward, not just scoring a point in this dispute.)

chapter 3

Step 1:
Awareness of
How You Communicate

$\mathcal{E}$very day and in every way, your teenager is unconsciously asking you the same question: "*Do you truly love me?*" And of course, you *do*. Otherwise, you wouldn't be taking the time and making the effort to read this book, you wouldn't be worrying about what kind of an adult he or she will turn out to be, and you wouldn't be driven up the wall by his or her often-outlandish behavior. If you didn't love your kid, you wouldn't care about him or her any more than you do about some other teen who lives down the street.

But, of course, your teen probably doesn't really ask directly, "Do you truly love me?" And you probably don't answer directly in words, either. Instead, your behavior—and the way you communicate—answers for you. And that's where the answer gets complicated . . . and critical.

Your actions should emphatically answer that unasked question with "*Yes!*" Because while words can be buoying, words can be warm and cuddly, and words can be welcome, it's *action* that largely communicates meaning for a teen. And how your actions answer the am-I-loved query pretty much determines your youngster's basic attitude toward life.

In this chapter I want to help hone your awareness of how you communicate with your words, of course, but also with your actions. Your overall manner of communicating is the conduit through which so much of your love is funneled. And your awareness of how you do is *so* important!

The purpose of communication

Relatively few teenagers are lucky enough to *feel* truly loved and accepted. They may actually be loved and accepted, but in many cases their parents falsely assume that they, the parents, clearly transmit those feelings. This is one of the biggest problems in families today: Parents don't know how to convey the love they feel; they don't know how to communicate it.

As I say, much of this communication is through action, not words. For example, one of the most important factors in how secure a teenager feels is the quality of his parents' marital relationship. It's folly to have a warring relationship with your spouse but try to convince your teen what you're all about is love and good wishes. In fact, perhaps the single best thing you can do for your child's emotional well-being is to really, really love your spouse—and *show* it in words and action.

For example, Bonnie shared with me that David, her 14-year-old, "all of a sudden" got his act together. He cleaned up his room, improved his grades, and was looking into what colleges to attend and what subjects to study. This contrasted greatly with David's earlier negativism in which he had been sullen and withdrawn for months. "He's a different boy. I hope it lasts," his mother said.

I got her to think about what else had changed that might have spurred David's new behavior. I was quite sure we were not witnessing what Bonnie called "a miracle," but instead the result of some changes we'd been working on in therapy.

The problem had been that Bonnie and her husband Walter were at odds. They barely talked to each other, let alone to their son. They got angry when they did try to discuss things with him or about him. Unable to share their feelings and emotions with one another, the parents never shared their expectations with their son, either.

When the father did assert himself, he'd try to be a buddy to David one moment, a strict disciplinarian the next. David would appeal to his mom, who would side with David and against the father in these disagreements, which often became heated. Nothing would get accomplished, and David would storm into his room and slam the door.

So he further demonstrated his anger by doing things that embarrassed and upset his parents, such as being slovenly, doing poorly in school, and refusing to discuss his future. Bonnie at first was unwilling to look at the possibility that her own issues with her husband needed to be addressed. Eventually, though, I was able to convince her that the lack of communication between herself and her husband was undermining effective parenting. I urged her to put all her efforts into strengthening the relationship with Walter. Talk about your expectations for one another and for your son, I urged, and come up with a united front about how to parent David rather than forcing him to choose sides.

To her credit, Mom rose to the challenge. She and her husband began communicating better, stopped undermining each other in front of their son, and were able to set reasonable boundaries for themselves and David. They effectively ended years of guerrilla warfare.

The point is, teenagers hunger for parents whose marital relationship is one of stability, love, and good communication, especially communication of unpleasant feelings. In times of stress, particularly, honest discussion—backed up by action—becomes critical for teens as well as parents.

A big difference

A big difference between adults and teens is that teens are behaviorally oriented while adults are more verbally oriented. A wife may be thrilled when a husband calls from work to tell her he loves her. If he calls to tell the teen the same thing, the kid probably will impatiently roll his or her eyes and wonder what's the real reason for the call.

So just saying "*I love you*" to a teen is fine and should be done. But it's not enough. Your teen judges your love by what you say and do, especially what you do. He is far more influenced by your actions than your words.

Teenagers are a lot like mirrors; they reflect what we send them. If love is given, they return it. If none is given, they don't. And conditional love is returned conditionally. And insincere words are expendable. Teens have a jugular instinct for what they judge to be false, to be phony.

That's a big reason it's important not to lose your self-control. Even if the teen does something outrageous, if you over-react and "go ballistic," if you call him or her names and say things you'll later regret, you'll lose a lot of hard-won respect, especially if it happens often. No amount of "I love you" happy talk compensates for a cursing, plate-throwing tantrum. The teen believes he has seen the "real" you and it isn't pretty. He rejects the "phony," nice you.

The right time for communicating

Choosing the right time and place for communicating with your teen is almost as important as choosing the words. The first rule: Don't try this when you're really angry. If you're a walking time bomb set to explode, you'll do no one any good.

Keep this in mind: Every hitch in a relationship, every thoughtless act or unkind word, every possibly misunderstood or ambiguous gesture doesn't need to be discussed immediately. Many laymen and some therapists urge debating every disagreement right on the spot when and where it occurs. I disagree.

There's no penalty for delay, as long as delay isn't an excuse for never bringing up the subject. And the benefit for a delay may be that you'll later be able to think more clearly about the incident and put it in perspective. Maybe it will even seem like a non-event, and not worth mentioning at all. Or more likely, it'll be worth mentioning but with the added context and thoughtfulness that time provides.

Be a Parent, Not a Pushover

Whatever you do, don't just get angry and say the first thing that comes to your mind. You can do a lot of damage to the relationship that way.

Before you spout off, ask yourself:

- Are my muscles clenched and tight? My heart pounding?
- Is my breathing shallow and rapid? My face hot and flushed?
- Are my thoughts racing and repeating? Do I feel anger and/or despair?
- Am I having an adrenaline rush?

If any of those conditions are present, you're probably in a fight or flight stage. This is not a good time to chat.

Similarly, if you observe your teen in an agitated state, back off. Talk tomorrow when everyone has calmed down. You'll be glad you did. Everyone's interests will be better served.

Remember, *you* are the adult. It's your responsibility to see that there is civilized communication.

The right setting for communication

Choosing the right place, too, is important. You want to make sure you'll have some time to talk without interruption. One of teens' most common complaints is that their parents talk to them as sort of an afterthought. The mother is peeling potatoes or the dad is listening to the ballgame while half-heartedly conducting a conversation that the kid, at least, thinks is important.

Taking a walk together is often a good idea or perhaps a drive to the country. Or even a restaurant where the service is notoriously slow and you can tell the waiter or waitress you need some time before you order. Then give the teen your full attention.

Wherever and whenever you choose to communicate, make sure you give your teen your total attention. This involves more than just making eye contact. Making eye contact doesn't require real sacrifice, but giving full attention does. Giving a teen your full, undivided attention suggests that he or she is truly loved, that he is valuable in his own right, that he is the most important person in the world to you.

Only total attention can make them feel they are special. And that's vital to the development of their self-esteem, to their ability to relate and love others. Dr. Ross Campbell in his classic *How to Really Love Your Teenager* says getting your total attention is the greatest need a teen has, though parents have a hard time recognizing this, let alone fulfilling the need.

Too many parents seem to think that the other things they do for their kids—such as doing them favors or giving them gifts—substitute for total attention. But while often good, these other things don't necessarily equate to total attention, though they are easier to give and take much less time. But teens don't feel their best or behave their best unless they receive your total attention. So it's not something that's just nice to give when it's comfortable to do so; it's required.

The teen does or doesn't want to talk?

The psychological defenses of moody teens are very high, and time is needed for them to be able to genuinely communicate and share with you what's really on their minds. Time is the magic ingredient.

Figuring out when a teen wants to have a heart-to-heart is sometimes opaque.

Often they'll only communicate with grunts during a moody period. This happens a lot. You can tell he or she is brooding about something, but no amount of small talk seems to be able to loosen his tongue. How to respond?

Well, the best you can hope for is to be available. Read the clues, and don't pepper him with questions (*What did you do at school today? . . . Who was there? . . . What went wrong?*) Instead, create an opportunity for him to communicate with you when he's comfortable doing so. Maybe say something like, *Count on me if you need to talk about something?"* or *"If you want to talk later, I'll be around."* Or *"I might like to take a walk later tonight? I could use some company. Join me if you like.*

These primitive states—such as withdrawal, non-communication, or sullenness—are defenses against pressures he feels. The pressures, for example, to be independent, to be fully accepted by his peers, to express himself sexually are strong but largely doomed to frustration at this age.

Teens, boys especially, often will go to great lengths to avoid making this talk become "a big production." Boys at this age tend to view warily anything smacking of feelings or psychology or "touchy-feely." Instead of badgering him with questions, try to spend a half-hour or so in a pleasant way that does not put pressure on him to communicate. Probably the defenses will slowly crumble, and eventually the two of you will be able to share thoughts and feelings.

All of us, including teens, like to have an escape outlet, a way to end the conversation if it starts to go badly for them. They like to feel they're in a position to leave if anger, ridicule, disappointment, or rejection begins to affect them. Thus, if they can become too uncomfortable, they can get out. That's why they sometimes pick the oddest moments to initiate a chat, say, a few minutes before they're scheduled to go out or shortly before guests are due to arrive.

So be alert to that tactic. Accommodate it if you can. The rewards could be great.

Or at other times, the teen may test your mood by use of a smoke screen. This usually involves dropping a piece of potentially upsetting information as a way of testing if you can be trusted with what's really on his mind. For instance, "Some of the kids are talking about staying out all night after the prom." If you overreact, the teen will assume your answer to the big question ("What if *I* wanted to stay out all night after the Prom?") will be the same.

If you're calm and in control, your teen may be encouraged to be more open and sharing. In response to what "some of the kids" are doing, you might say. "That's interesting. Tell me what you think the pros and cons are about doing that?" or "Prom Night is special. But what do you think? Is there any big advantage to staying out all night as opposed to, say, 1 a.m.? If you feel strongly about it, that's something we could discuss."

A common preamble to these deeper conversations may be "Oh, by the way" or some equivalent. Like "Oh, by the way, some of the kids are going to Las Vegas next month." What that may really mean is: "The real reason I'm here is to sound you out about a more liberalized policy about unchaperoned trips."

So look for "Oh, by the way . . . " or "Hey, you know what?" as possible transition between smoke screen and real topic. So you need to be alert for the "feeling us out" process, testing in effect to see what mood you are in and if it's okay to approach.

A third way they may segue into a deeper conversation and disguise their own conflicts is talking about another teen who is purportedly having similar problems. Such as "There's this girl at school who supposedly slept with this boy and . . . " This can be a way to talk about awkward, embarrassing or difficult-to-handle situations.

Giving full attention

Once a potentially sensitive issue comes out, it's sometimes tempting for parents to make light of it with a casual or flippant reply. But you shouldn't do that. Even if the problem seems no big deal or something we can't do anything about, you should let them talk about it and give them your full attention. That will help cement the relationship regardless of what effect it has on the current issue.

Often the teen will just hint that he wants your affection or attention. For example, he or she may approach you and talk about some very superficial subject, say, the new kind of shoelaces some of the other kids are wearing these days. But she seems so intense and serious and strangely out of context, given the nature of the subject matter. At that time it's important to be patient. The teen is stalling until her defenses can come down so that she can talk about something more important, perhaps how she feels out of step with the other kids in general or how high school is putting uncommon pressures or her, or something.

Be careful not to cut her off (*"Who cares about shoestrings, for God's sake? That's not important!"*) because that would likely be seen as rejection. Be patient and give her the time she needs; be an active listener.

Messages—nonverbal

Eye contact and physical contact are an important part of communicating. These should be part of our everyday dealings. A child whose parents use eye and physical contact will likely be more comfortable with himself and others, be a better communicator, and have better self-esteem.

Eye contact, especially, is a little gesture whose presence or absence can covey big meaning. There's surprisingly little eye contact in many households and when it does exist it's usually negative, such as when the teen is being reprimanded. The more you can make eye contact in a loving way, the more your teen will feel nourished.

By physical contact, I mean lightly touching in an appropriate, consistent way to give the teen the feeling that you really care. This can be especially helpful when the teen is sullen, moody or resistant, and thus unlikely to respond well to words alone. A light, brief touch on the arm as you pass by, or a little squeeze on the shoulder before he or she leaves for school can speak volumes. You can also give longer, more intense hugs or shoulder squeezes or handclasps from time to time.

Be a Parent, Not a Pushover

The teen, of course, wants and needs such contact. But as true of much about teen behavior, there is a push-pull mechanism at work here. Teens both want something (such as love, freedom, and decision-making power) and loathe it. That's part of the birth pangs of independence.

In this case, sure, he wants affection because it shows you care and he is wanted . . . and he rejects it because he wants to also see himself or herself as an adult who doesn't need such attention. (That adults also need this kind of physical contact isn't yet a fact he understands.)

So sometimes the teen may not be able to consciously accept your touch because he's in his hyper-independent mode and just may not be relating to you. Even so, you can give physical contact when his attention is diverted so that he may be unaware that you're about to touch him. It will still register and let him know that he's cared for even when he's being difficult.

For instance, in the previous chapter you met Laurie and her difficult son, Jamie. Laurie said her family situation improved when she learned to manage her anger and not engage in escalating verbal duels with Jamie. But that didn't mean everything was perfect. Jamie still suffered from poor self-esteem and felt "second best" when it came to his younger brother.

Once Laurie knew Jamie's anger stemmed from resentment about his brother, she continued to look for new approaches. One technique she discovered was that when she sensed an argument over something "meaningless" was about to start, she would walk up to Jamie and say, "You could really use a hug right now." That, she told me, helped a lot to defuse the tense situation.

You probably know your teen well enough to know how much physical contact he or she can accept without recoiling. And of course if the teen has soreness or aches from sports injuries or roughhousing, that's a good excuse to give physical contact, too.

Should you hug and kiss? Well, sure. But you don't want to do it so much as to make him feel uncomfortable. But there are times when it's appropriate, such as leaving or returning from a trip, say, or winning an award or accomplishing some long-sought goal. Or perhaps when he comes to you deeply hurt or troubled and needs consoling.

Sometimes it's hard to tell when the teen needs physical contact, and he or she may be unable to tell you. So you should be alert for such opportunities. Avoid, though, making a physical gesture in front of his friends or in a public place. Though you may genuinely feel the emotion, the potential for embarrassment is probably just too high, unless your teen initiates it first.

Messages—verbal

You probably think you're a pretty good conversationalist, and you're probably right. But take a moment to ask yourself if you talk to your teen using open-ended versus dead-ended questions. The latter require just a "yes" or "no" answer. That's economical but not very enlightening.

Which is more typical of your conversations?

You: *Did you have a good day at school?*
Kid: *It was O.K.*

Be a Parent, Not a Pushover

End of conversation.

— or —

You: *Don't I remember that today was the day for the try-outs for the chess team? Did that come off as scheduled? How did that go?*

Let's say he or she responds by saying he didn't make the team and is disappointed. You could follow up by responding:

That must be tough playing under the coach's scrutiny like that. Were you nervous?
Do you agree with the coach's decision?
Will you try out again next year?
If you and I play a lot this year would that help you for next year?
Hmmm. Sounds as if you're disappointed but determined to work to improve. Is that right?

None of these responses would have likely followed if you just asked the dead-ended question, "Was school O.K. to-day?" and you would have missed an opportunity to have a more in-depth exchange. Remember, a real conversation gets two people involved, not just going through the motions.

Avoiding the dirty dozen

Some means of communicating are just plain wrong. They're incendiary and make any bad situation worse. Whatever you do, try to avoid these communication no-no's:

Step 1: Awareness

1. Blaming

This involves using the accusatory *you,* as in *"You are so lazy you make me sick."* Such a negative evaluation then becomes an issue when the real issue is you want the kid to clean up his or her room. By blaming, you've escalated the dispute to something more than just an untidy room; now it's a character defect that's being debated.

2. Name-calling

Stop acting stupid! or *You're a jerk, you know that?* again takes the focus off the behavior in question and elevates it to a personal attack. This is akin to throwing gasoline on the fire rather than trying to extinguish it.

3. Denying the importance of others' feelings

Parents too often say something like, *I know how you feel, but . . . .* You may not know how they feel. Or maybe you really do, but by denying the teen the opportunity to state or re-state those feelings, you're positioning yourself as a know-it-all who doesn't want to listen and perhaps doesn't really care.

4. Using sarcasm

That was really a smart thing to do . . . DUH! This is demeaning and does little to further communication.

5. Getting off the track

And, one more thing: You treated your sister badly at the picnic last year, too. Or *And how 'bout that time three weeks ago when you left jelly smears on the counter?* We can't correct all problems at once. Throwing too many issues and sore points into a discussion just ensures that none of them will be fully addressed.

6. Making crying an offense

Don't start crying—or I'll really give you something to cry about, parents often say. But crying is a valid response to some situations. A teen who cries in front of a parent is exposing his or her vulnerability. That's not easy for either party, so respect their loss.

7. Preaching or moralizing

Using *shoulds* and *oughts* in talk with a teen is like brandishing a cross in front of a vampire; it stops the dialogue in its tracks. Instead, try teaching, not preaching.

8. Commanding

A common parental failing, issuing commands (*Clean your room, Get dressed, Get up on time for once*), becomes a habit. So does ignoring them.

9. Teasing

Like sarcasm, teasing, or making fun of your kid, devalues the child. Of course, there's nothing wrong with poking a little fun at human foibles, whether adult or adolescent. But when it becomes habitual and/or cruel, teasing closes down the avenues of communication. At such times teasing *becomes* the problem instead of helping to solve it.

10. Over-catastrophizing

Keep that up and you're going to be a homeless person living in a cardboard box or *You can't do one single solitary thing right in your whole life.* Sure, you exaggerate for effect. But it stings and impedes problem solving.

11. Using "You are . . ." messages

You constantly are interrupting me with your half-baked opinions, or *You never keep your promises.* Habitually using "you are" makes every statement an accusation and puts the other person on the defensive. Instead, try *I feel . . .* and *I wish . . .* statements, such as *I feel frustrated when I can't finish what I want to say* or *I wish we could agree on what we're going to do and then stick to it. Can we?*

12. Committing violence

A thrown object, a push, a slap . . . or worse. This is the most destructive of all roadblocks to communication. It is *never* acceptable.

Defensive pessimism

Another technique you can use to your advantage in communicating with your teen is what's known as defensive pessimism. Although it sounds depressing, it's not just for those who adopt a negative outlook. To the contrary, it can actually be elevating by helping you prepare for what you fear could become a difficult round of verbal combat. Defensive pessimism thus can be both self-protective and motivational, a useful tool for parents to harness their power and remain flexible and solution-focused.

Let's say your 17-year-old son comes home from a party, and you know that he has been drinking. You can smell the alcohol, and he is obviously high. If you are like most parents, the urge will be to confront him right then. But this is not the time to get into an argument; his safety is really the first consideration. This will require your detachment, or non-attachment, which I'll describe in more detail later.

We know that teens do not metabolize alcohol as quickly as adults and can get into a toxic state after falling asleep. Alcohol poisoning can result in disability and even death. So the best thing that you can do is to keep him up for a while to ensure his safety.

The time to talk to him is the next day when he has sobered up. That's when you should express your disappointment and disapproval. You may expect him to react with anger and defiance. So instead of just rushing headlong into the dispute, take a few moments to imagine his responses. That's where defensive pessimism comes in. You know him pretty well, and you probably can come up with some worst-case scenarios of what he's likely to say. *I don't need you to boss me around. I'm not taking orders from you anymore,* he might reply. Or perhaps *You think I drink too much? That's a laugh, seeing how loaded you get every Saturday night, you hypocrite.*

If you have these kinds of rejoinders in your head, you can better respond to them calmly. You can figure out what would be the best, most non-inflammatory reply. Thus, you can lower your outrage if he does say these hurtful things.

And if he *doesn't*, you'll be relieved. In either event, you'll be preparing for the worst and hoping for the best, which is always a good strategy.

Set your boundaries and discuss with him what will happen if he repeats this behavior. Don't presume that it won't happen again. In fact, if your teen continues to abuse alcohol or drugs, you should contact a substance abuse counselor. Together, you can find out what's really happening and begin to set guidelines and consequences. Discussing consequences and results teaches teens that what happens to them in life is a result of what they do.

When it gets to the stage where outside help is needed, parents tend to "cave in" because the consequences can be severe. In the above case, the teen may need to go into a treatment center, essentially leaving home, which is a difficult decision for most parents. If you are attached to the outcome—attached to the idea that your kid *must* cooperate and change—you reduce your flexibility and your ability to help generate change. Non-attachment allows you to remain loving and accepting while trying to solve the problem. This example may be extreme because we know most teens are tougher on themselves than parents might expect. But they will test limits.

Handling strong emotional reactions

A more subtle way to handle such conflict is to seek to disengage yourself from your emotional reaction. Then—rather than just reacting—explain your feelings to your teen, along with a proposed solution.

Be a Parent, Not a Pushover

Here's how this method works: When the teen's behavior triggers a strong emotional reaction in you, direct your focus inside your body and notice how this emotion feels. Give this emotion a name, such *This is anger*, or *This feels like betrayal*.

Recognize that you are *not* your feelings. They are distinct from you, and you can watch them wax and wane. One of my favorite sayings to my clients is, "Your feelings have no brains. So you need to learn to not react to them."

With practice, you'll be able to decide what feelings you will tolerate and which you will ignore. Think specifically about what your teen did to cause this particular emotion. Finally, share with him or her what you learned by thinking this through and how you would wish he would act. Then offer to help solve the problem in a way that'll help the relationship.

This takes self-control and thoughtful effort, but it pays off. You may even wish to write down the steps. For example, let's say the problem is that your daughter disobeys by staying out later than she's allowed.

Instead of just yelling at her and demanding that she return home earlier, you might approach it this way:

When you stay out so late, I feel very upset. I get very worried because you might be in trouble or even in danger. I wish you would return home on time or at least call to let me know your schedule if you're going to be late. If you will promise to do that, I'll promise to relax the deadline and not be on your case so much about staying out late. Together, we can accomplish both of our goals: You can have more freedom, and I can have less worry about someone I really love.

Notice that this is an assertive—but not an accusatory—style of communicating.

First, you tell them how you feel when they act in a certain way. Then you suggest how they could act differently and how you will try to make it easier for them to act differently. Finally, you indicate how this new behavior will improve the relationship.

Try it.

Honing your listening skills

It's been said that we listen more than we do any other human activity, except breathe. And most of us probably think we're better listeners than we are.

But you've probably been at a dinner or a party where you got the impression no one was really listening. Rather, they were all just rehearsing what they might say next. Maybe they were thinking about how to sound good, how to effectively make their points, or how to outscore the others. As a result, by evening's end, everyone had spoken—but no one had communicated much or gotten to know anyone else very well.

Unfortunately, many of our everyday conversations with our teens are like that. While we *hear*, we only pretend to listen. Listening doesn't just mean shutting up while someone else speaks, though that's a start. But listening—*real* listening—takes more work than that. It requires an intellectual and emotional effort as well.

To get a full appreciation of your teen and what's being said, you need to interpret body language, ask questions, give feedback, remain objective, and figure out what's really being said and what's not being said. As Matthew McKay and Martha Davis say in their book, *How To Communicate*, "Listening is a commitment and a compliment. It's a commitment to understanding how other people feel, how they see their world." Moreover, "it's a compliment because it says to the other person: 'I care about what's happening to you. Your life and your experience are important to me.'"

Learning to listen better can help transform your relationship with your teen by making him or her feel appreciated, by increasing trust, and by helping to solve problems more quickly. If you're going to give your teen your *full attention*, as I described earlier, you're going to need to become a good listener.

And to become a better listener, you're going to need to reduce or eliminate both physical and psychological barriers. Physically, you're going to want to minimize distractions so you can pay attention. You might turn off the TV or the radio, or put away your magazine. Take a deep breath (this will prevent you from interrupting *and* provide your brain with invigorating oxygen.) And maintain eye contact as you consciously decide to listen.

Further, you will want to acknowledge what your teen is saying. You can do that by gestures such as smiling, nodding your head, leaning forward with interest, and using other facial expressions and body language. You also can acknowledge him or her with verbal responses or vocal participation, such as "*Hmm,*" "*I see,*" or "*Yeah.*" These all state: "I'm interested in what you have to say."

Asking questions, giving feedback, and making comments at the appropriate time is also an essential part of active listening. It simplifies the listener's job by getting the speaker to open up, perhaps reveal hidden feelings, motives, and goals.

As I mentioned earlier, it's very important not to overreact emotionally when your teen is speaking. When your emotional reaction begins, you'll have an almost irresistible tendency to interrupt or to argue. You'll feel your pulse and your breathing speed up. But you should take a deep breath and imagine yourself calm and relaxed. When you exercise such emotional control, you'll find that active listening is no longer a struggle.

Sense the nonverbal message

In addition to listening, it's important that you read the nonverbal messages in any communications. If you don't, you may miss a major aspect of his message.

Be alert to his—and *your*—body language. What the two of you do with your eyes, face, hands, arms, legs, and posture sends out signals as to whether you are, or aren't, listening and understanding what the other person is saying.

For instance, if you were speaking and the person you were talking to was glancing sideways, sighing, looking at the ceiling, fidgeting in the chair, or cracking his knuckles, you'd deduce that no matter what words come from this person's mouth, he or she actually has zero interest in what you're talking about and wishes you'd just go away.

Conversely, if your partner were looking you in the eyes, raising his eyebrows periodically, licking his lips, tilting his head, and leaning toward you, he would be showing interest in you and in what you're saying. The point is, when you acknowledge the other person both verbally and nonverbally, you build trust and increase rapport.

Abstain from judging

One of the toughest things to do when we speak to our teens is not to prejudge them or what they're about to say. When you prejudge, you automatically cease paying real attention to what they're saying. So a basic rule of listening is to judge only after you've heard and evaluated what they say. Try not to jump to conclusions.

Instead, try to listen with empathy. No matter how outrageous, inconsiderate, false, or self-centered the teen may seem at that moment, remember: he or she is simply trying to survive, just like you. We're all participating in roughly the same physical and psychological struggle. Some of us just have more experience and better survival strategies than others.

So cut your kid some slack for being young and inexperienced. So listening with empathy means asking yourself, *"Where is this person's anger coming from?" "What is he or she really asking for?" "What can I do that's reasonable and non-condemning?"* Genuinely listening well is, at its heart, a healing act of love.

Really listening, in short, means concentrating on the other person's words and meaning rather than formulating your own response before they've even finished.

Learning to be an active listener is like learning to swim or jog. It takes effort. You start little by little and work upward.

It's as much a state of mind as a physical activity. But as you improve, it pays ever-increasing rewards.

Lessons Learned

The most effective way to get something you need from others is to give it freely yourself. Thus, a key to getting your teen to communicate is by being a good communicator (speaker and listener) yourself. Take the time and make the effort to have your teen believe he or she has your full attention and is *really* being heard. You'll likely find that in return he or she is more willing to listen to you.

Keep in mind that your teen gets relationship clues from how he sees his mother and father relate. If the spouses are angry and antagonistic, it's a safe bet the teen will reflect that. So, please, if not for your sake, then for your kid's sake, be slow to anger, quick to forgive, and work hard at making that spousal relationship the best it can be.

With your teen *and* with your spouse, avoid losing your temper and saying things that hurt. Teens judge more by actions than words. If you try to project a lovey-dovey image but then periodically erupt in wrath, the teen will judge the latter mood to be closer to the truth and won't trust your affection.

Try to choose the right time and place for your deep talks. You don't need to dissect every discordant note, every minor disagreement, precisely when it occurs and when emotions are roiling. Store the issue away, then bring it up later when passions have subsided.

To get you and your teen in the habit of deep communicating, try using open-ended questions that can't be answered with a "yes," "no," or a shrug. Be assertive, but not accusatory, in trying to come up with solutions to your disagreements. And seek to improve your listening skills. When you really start hearing each other, then perhaps you can begin to solve your differences instead of fighting over them.

chapter 4

Step 2: Direction— Giving Teens What They Need

*G*iving direction to your teen is a lot like driving down a really steep street. You know your car is going to pick up speed; that's gravity at work. And you know your teen is going to test his or her limits; that's human nature at work.

The key with both car and kid is to *control* that rate of speed: Let it—whether descent or independence—happen, but guide it so that something really disastrous doesn't occur.

Now if your car is old and has iffy brakes, you're going to approach that hill more cautiously. Maybe you'll come to a complete stop at the top so that you don't have much momentum. Or perhaps you'll hug the curb so you can make an emergency stop if need be. Or maybe you'll get the brakes fixed before you even dare to take on that incline.

Similarly, your teen's maturity will be a gauge for how quickly, how freely you grant him or her independence. To what degree can you trust your youngster and his ability to control his behavior? The answer will govern the degree of direction he or she needs.

Giving direction is a major stumbling block for many parents. They set the limits too tight or too loose. Set too tight, the limits may contribute to a teen's resentment at being needlessly hobbled. Set too loose, they may make the teen feel cut adrift or uncared for.

Some parents compound the problem by punishing infractions inconsistently. Or quarreling among themselves about how to set and enforce the rules.

In this chapter, we're going to look at some of the factors governing direction and help you find a balance that's right for your teen.

❦

The truth is, there are a lot of wimpy parents. They don't trust their own judgment. They treat their kids as if they are delicate crystal that might shatter with even the gentlest handling instead of fairly durable glassware that's designed to hold up pretty well if not abused.

But here's what you've got to keep in mind: You know more than your children—*and you're supposed to tell them what to do.* You weren't created to be their pals, their playmates, their servants. You've got more experience and better judgment—use it!

What's more—and trust me on this—all teens, at some level, know they need guidance from their parents. In fact, they want it. They're probably not going to admit that. To do so would be too much of a concession, too big of a blow to their youthful egos. But in their heart of hearts, they know they're still a kid in a scary grownup world. They like the reassurance that comes with knowing there's somebody who cares for and looks after them.

Setting and testing limits

Just accept the fact that it's normal for a teen to test and sometimes break whatever limits you set. If you come up with a midnight curfew, you can almost bet that before long he or she will try coming back at 12:15 or 12:30. And if that goes unchallenged, 12:45, then 1 a.m.

What's that tell us? In the beginning, make the rules very strict. Then as the child matures and shows he or she can be trusted, you can gradually ease the restrictions. It's always more pleasant for you to be the good guy and add privileges rather than be the bad guy and take them away. And it's better for both sides if you can relax the rules because of good actions, not tighten them because of poor behavior.

Further, as Dr. Ross Campbell points out in his excellent *How to Really Love Your Teenager,* if you initially set the standards too loose and the teen breaks them, he's more likely to harm or disgrace himself than if you set them tight at the beginning and he broke them. Most teens get their driver's license, for example, at age 16. Naturally, once they're "official" in the eyes of the state motor vehicles department, they want to drive everywhere at all times and in all conditions.

That's legal, but is it wise? Probably not. Yes, they're licensed, but are they experienced at driving, say, in fog or rain or other inclement conditions? Are they mature enough to drive home in the wee hours in a car full of boisterous partygoers? Are they checked out enough to drive alone to a remote desert location or through dangerous mountain passes? You probably will want to see their driving résumé broadened before okaying those kinds of automotive adventures.

Similarly, "Better safe than sorry" is probably a good motto to follow as you set somewhat strict limits on other sorts of activities. Then you can ease the rules once you're sure the teen has the maturity and the sense of responsibility to handle them.

Strength and courage required

But, understand, it takes strength of will to set and stick with rules. One of the reasons so many parents wimp out and set weak rules, or none at all, is because they lack courage of their convictions. They know they'll get pressured. The teen will push for a relaxation of the rules without having earned that. Other teens will lobby them to ease up because "all the kids" are doing something or other. Other parents may suggest that the stricter parents are out of step. Even society itself may seem arrayed against them. But if the parents have thought through the rules and those rules fit the plan, they should stick with them.

Another reason parents waffle on setting realistic limits is that they want their kid to love and admire them. That's a worthy goal, but it's wrongheaded to think that leniency is going to achieve it. In fact, there's some reason to believe just the opposite. Some kids, very quick to perceive weakness, may counter with, "If you loved me, you'd let me stay out 'til 4 a.m. like Jamie's folks allow her to do." Or, "I hate you because you're so strict." Parents need to have enough self-confidence to see through such fleeting—maybe even contrived—anger and stick to well-reasoned rules.

My advice: If you know you've been fair and reasonable in setting limits, then gut it out. After all, you're the grownup here. And this, too, shall pass. The teen eventually will come around to see the logic of you making some rules, even if he or she doesn't always agree with the specifics.

Maybe you didn't have a very good relationship with your own parents. Perhaps they were too strict, and you suffered as a result. Maybe you or they, or both, have some guilt at not having gotten along, of not having come up with a division of power that worked for both parties. But that was then and this is now. Don't repeat their mistake by going to the other extreme. Give your kid a reasonable structure: Tough at first, then progressively more liberal as his or her behavior dictates.

What's the goal?

After all, what's the aim here? It's not for you to be praised every moment or earn a Parent of the Year award. The aim is to turn your teen into an independent adult who makes good decisions. In fact, a really good idea might be for you to state clearly that very point to your teen: *Our goal here is to help you become a responsible, independent adult who can set his own rules. The more that you show me that you are responsible, the more independence I can give you. Is that a deal?*

Stating it that way—and following through—may help the teen see the logic of the rules and get him or her invested in the process. Rather than having the limits forced on him arbitrarily, he can see their purpose and can work almost as your teammate toward that day when such limits will be unnecessary.

You could develop this sense of teamwork in a lot of ways. Take money, for instance. Maybe the teen complains that she doesn't have enough compared to other kids, that her allowance is too paltry, that she doesn't have credit cards like some of the other teens, and that, in effect, you're a tightwad.

You could, first, explain the importance of adult money management and how you want to help her achieve that skill. Then maybe you could give her some added chores, with the money going into a checking account accessible by a debit card. That way she couldn't spend more than what she had in the account, and she'd be responsible for replenishing it. And tell her that if she handles that well for a year or so, you might consider getting her a credit card, especially if she ends up going to college.

In fact, talking a lot about the future, such as college or a full-time job, is probably a good idea. Even if the discussion is with, say, a 14- or 15-year-old and thus must be couched in general terms, talking about the future reinforces the idea that you're working together toward a time of independence. Thus, it gives a context for your rules: Someday, those restrictions will disappear *if the teen is ready*. That's a powerful incentive for cooperation.

Filling the vacuum

Many parents reading this book grew up in the 1960s or '70s when "Go with the flow" was the mantra. Structure was out, spontaneity was in. We were a new generation, and by God, we were going to be *free!* Sure, we shook off the bonds of conformity. But what did we replace them with?

Too often we let go of the philosophies and rituals that families need. And it's rituals, values, and standards that instill honor, dignity, and cooperation. (See Chapter 7 for more about family rituals, what they can accomplish, and how you can create them.)

Others, though, are quick to fill any vacuum left by the family. Today's pop culture—including TV, music, movies, and the Internet—is edgy and vulgar. And have you seen the video games with their bloody, violent graphics? Sometimes I think the whole country's asleep but our children are awake. Because no one takes accountability for what these forms of media are doing to our kids, you must be responsible for your teen.

For example, adolescents who watch more than three hours of TV daily are more likely to engage in aggressive behavior as adults, according to a study at Columbia University. About 29% of those who watched three or more hours daily of TV at age 14 had engaged in assaults or other aggressive behavior by age 22. These researchers tracked 700 youth for 17 years and concluded that—even after accounting for factors such as family income, neglect, or mental disorders—the link between watching violent television and becoming aggressive adults was clear.

Hundreds of studies in more than a dozen countries have all come to a similar conclusion: Children who watch violent television programs behave more aggressively than those who do not. There's no longer any real debate in the scientific community about this relationship. Professional health organizations such as the American Academy of Pediatrics, America Psychological Association, and American Medical Association all have concluded there is a link between extensive TV viewing and aggression in young people.

Yet adolescents spend on average 22 hours a week watching TV (and some as many as *60 hours!*)—that's *ridiculous*. Passive consumption of commercial television also can lead to attention deficits, poor decision-making, and even obesity.

Clear and consistent rule-making

Parents who establish rules of behavior have better relationships with their teens—and a significantly lower incidence of smoking, drinking, and using illegal drugs by the teen. That's the conclusion of a study (also mentioned in Chapter 2) of 1,000 teens by The National Center on Addiction and Substance Abuse, part of its annual national teen substance abuse survey.

The study compared a "hands-on" versus a "hands-off" approach. It found that only one in four teens has "hands-on" parents,. But those teens are at only one-quarter the risk for drug abuse than those living in "hands-off" households. ("Hands-on" was defined as parents who consistently take 10 or more of 12 specific actions, such as monitoring what their teens watch on TV and the Internet, restricting what CDs they buy, imposing a curfew, assigning chores to the teen, and so on.)

You'll likely forge a better long-term relationship with your teen if you come up with strict rules and enforce them than if you don't. Sure, there may be some short-term grumbling. But over the long haul, the teen will know you really care and will respect you for investing time and effort in the rule-setting process, especially if you are calm, consistent, and give positive feedback.

Let's look further at those points:

Calmness

The more pleasant your relationship with your teen, the better he or she will accept your rules. But if you have a sour history to start with, if you are easily angered or abusive, you're going to meet resistance on every point. Even wholly logical limits may be resisted—and defied—because to do otherwise would be to grant you a point in this ongoing grudge match. The answer, of course, is to not let a grudge match arise in the first place.

You need a reservoir of goodwill to get anybody to do almost anything. To the extent you have developed such a reservoir and have avoided anger, you should be able to develop that "team" approach we spoke of. Choose a good time to talk and calmly explain the rules, perhaps along these lines:

> *You're getting to that age where, say, you're going to be invited to a lot of parties. I want you to go and enjoy yourself and expand socially; that's a part of growing up. But not all parties are created equal, and some unsupervised gatherings where drugs or alcohol are available are likely to be more than you can or should be asked to handle right now. Maybe later when you're fully an adult, but not now.*

Be a Parent, Not a Pushover

So until you're fully confident in such situations—and until I have peace of mind about this—we need to come up with some rules. Here is what I think they should be:

1. *No parties without at least a week's notice.*
2. *I need to be told where the event will be held and the name and phone number of the responsible parent.*
3. *You will call home at least once during the party and again before you leave.*
4. *You'll be home no later than midnight.*
5. *You won't ride with anyone who's been drinking or using drugs.*
6. *You promise not to drink alcohol or use drugs of any kind.*
7. *If you violate any of these rules, party privileges will be suspended for at least one month.*
8. *In a year, we'll revisit these rules and make changes as necessary.*

Do those rules make sense to you? Do you see the rationale for them?

Work with me on these, and we can loosen them as time goes by.

Or, something like that. No ultimatum. No name-calling or expressions of distrust. No moralizing or preaching from a superior to a subordinate. No getting locked into a power struggle. Instead, you, the senior partner, take the lead, explain why rules are necessary, and what the game plan will be for implementing them and eventually phasing them out.

Step 2: Direction

Consistency

Few things are as disturbing to a teen as parental inconsistency, especially about matters that the parents say they highly value but then treat as a trifle. The adults may say they value honesty, but then lie to their spouse or cheat on their taxes. They may lay claim to morality, but then defraud others in business. They may give lip service to selflessness, then manipulate family members for their own gain. Teens really do learn by what we do, not what we say. What lesson are you teaching?

Similarly, even if the parents do practice what they preach, too often they're not steadfast in how they enforce the rules. They waffle, speaking sternly and setting firm limits one moment, and then rolling over the next.

If your teen disobeys the rules, punish him or her as you promised. Not to do so is to weaken your word. You need to demonstrate the imperative of accountability. That is, you need to show them a major life lesson: Making choices brings consequences—and bad choices bring bad consequences. You must show how you take ownership of results.

A friend of mine recalls seeing a nautical speed limit sign at the entrance to a harbor and the warning: "Boats are responsible for their own wake." So, too, are we responsible for what follows in our wake. Make it really clear that your teen's actions govern outcomes.

And make it a point to own up to your own consequences, too. Avoid getting into the "blame game' and wrapping yourselves or others in the cloak of "victim." Blame is irrelevant.

Be a Parent, Not a Pushover

You want to teach your teens—and exemplify in your personal dealings—that we all are participants in our lives and in the lives of others, and we have some influence on the results in both cases. Don't blame others for your misfortunes. Explain to your teen where you've succeeded and failed and how you hope to do better. And encourage them to accept accountability, too.

Another inconsistency occurs when the spouses disagree among themselves about discipline. Mom, for instance, may think the son should be able to go swimming with his friends at the quarry until midnight but Dad doesn't. Husband and wife don't need to agree on every point or every situation—but they need to concur on the broad outlines of how rules will be set and enforced. Negotiation and compromise will be required.

Parents, even if separated or divorced, need to have a system for deciding what to do when they disagree among themselves. For example, a possible compromise in this situation: The son can go this time *if* he's back by 11. Or he can't go swimming at the quarry, but he can do something else he's been pushing for.

Parents need to form a united front, and each should be careful not to undercut the other. Kids become quite expert at driving wedges between their parents when they sense a division. If the teen is asking something of you but not your spouse, be cautious. You might say, "You raise a good point about that camping trip to Mexico. I don't feel comfortable making a decision without talking to your mom (or dad). Let me do that and get back to you." And parents definitely should never argue about discipline in front of the teens. At best, that's confusing to the teen. At worst, it encourages him or her to play one parent against the other.

Positive feedback

Catch your teen doing something right. Congratulate her, for instance, for making an extra effort on her chores, for calling you when you asked her to, for having the backbone not to drink or smoke when her friends are doing so. Encourage your teens in their areas of competence, whether it's playing the piano or just being a good-natured person.

You want to be a person from whom your teen gathers strength. He or she will derive that strength from your acknowledgment and support. Too many parents concentrate on telling their kids how they must change instead of praising them for behaving well or being helpful. Look for the good in your teen. It's there. And the more you find it and reward it, the more it's likely to multiply.

A poisoned well?

A teamwork approach to giving direction may make sense if you have something of a reservoir of goodwill with your teen, if there's basically respect between the two of you. But what if there's not? What if the well is already poisoned?

Then you've got a lot of work to do beyond setting rules. To begin with, you need to, as the previous chapter suggested, work really hard on your communication skills. Then, as we'll discuss further in Chapter 10, learn to harness your own anger. But for now, ask yourself: *"Have I been taking anger about my job or my marriage out on my teen?"* You may want to revisit Chapter 2, "Parent, Know Thyself."

And remember, if you want to change someone else, the best place to start is by changing yourself.

What should you require of your teen?

Specifically, how can you give intelligent direction? Well, for starters, there's no way around it: You've got to get involved. Spend time with your teens. Ask questions. Listen to the answers. Observe. Then come up with some rules.

You don't want to treat them like tiny children. But you do want to make it clear that you're still in charge. Don't unconditionally approve or accept everything your teen does. Remind them—*and* yourself—that saying "no" can be an act of love.

Also, try to give a reason for every rule. Don't just say, *Because I've decided that's the way it's going to be!* or *I just know better!* Emphasize your love for them, what your concern is about the activity, and why this rule will help the teen become an independent adult.

Don't be lured into debating the rule. Just state your rationale; it's important to always give a reason. Then say what the rule will be. Ask for the teen's reaction, of course; accept feedback. But resist the idea of arguing the pros and cons.

Most teens have, I believe, a sense of fairness. They may not praise you for putting restrictions on them. But at some level, they acknowledge the rightness of reasonable rules— especially if you leave open the possibility of phasing out the rules as the teen proves his or her maturity and judgment.

Step 2: Direction

Some further ideas to govern rule-making:

Know what your kids are seeing and hearing in the media

Monitor what they're watching on TV and seeing on the Internet—and don't be shy about questioning whether that's appropriate. Check out their video games, too, and what CDs they buy. (Invite your teen to play his or her favorite CD in the car while you're driving. I predict: You'll be amazed at what you hear!)

Set limits on television viewing

Restrict TV-watching, perhaps setting a limit of a certain number of hours per night. Or perhaps no TV on school nights, during dinner, or just before bedtime. Consider making the teen's bedroom a "no-TV" zone because when you put a TV in his or her room, you give up control over viewing habits.

Watch some TV with your teen. That's how you can learn about their favorite shows. That also gives you a chance to voice your opinion so they can understand your values and judgment.

Talk with your teen about the "opportunity cost" of TV—all the other things you or the teen could be doing instead of watching television. And get in the habit of "talking back" to your TV ("Now is drinking that soda really going to make you or me sexy?"), and discuss advertisers' tricks with your teens ("What is that commercial really trying to sell me? How does it try to do so—with music, sex, celebrities, tricks, or what?").

Be a Parent, Not a Pushover

Make it clear that there's more to life than marketing

The average child sees more than 20,000 commercials a year, according to the American Academy of Pediatrics. Total advertising in this country amounts to about $100 billion a year, which is almost $400 for every single person.

Some of this we need to make decisions about our life. But when ads appear everywhere all the time, it's time to take a hike, literally and otherwise. Don't let your kids get hopelessly sucked into the belief that TV networks or snack companies or designers of sportswear determine what is real.

You don't need to accept the view that there's nothing you can do to combat rampant commercialism. Yes, it's a part of American life. But it doesn't need to be an unlimited part. Have you ever glanced at the number of items in your child's belongings that have corporate logos or stars' names on them? It's hard to find almost anything that *doesn't*.

Not one of those is automatically bad, but cumulatively, there's a tremendous negative impact. Advertisers seek to hook young consumers as early as possible. Children are particularly vulnerable because they sometimes have difficulty distinguishing between reality and fantasy. Ads come to define their reality and are often indistinguishable from the television programs. Those ads for $150 sneakers and endless toys, gifts, and gadgets link happiness with consumption and can shape kids' values in ways you would not wish. Consumption becomes an end unto itself. Thus, the need to have the right jeans, the right designer t-shirt, and the right watch supplant the need to do the right thing or be a good person.

Step 2: Direction

Commercialism isn't going to disappear. So you can forget about avoiding it, but you can try to minimize its effects. How? Here are some ideas:

- Take the time and make the effort to get your teen familiar with nature, with animals, with the joys associated with real people and real situations, not just those created on a Hollywood sound stage.
- Try to encourage purchases of items that don't have logos.
- Get acquainted with non-profit groups that share the goal of keeping commercialism in check. For example:

Center for a New American Dream
6930 Carroll Ave., Suite 900
Takoma Park, MD 20912
(301)891-ENUF
www.newdream.org

CNAD is a 4,500-member organization that seeks to lessen materialism as a way of protecting the environment. It offers "Tips for Parenting in a Commercial Culture" as well as a "Turn the Tide" program of individual, environmentally-friendly actions.

National Institute on Media and the Family
606 24th Ave. So., No. 600
Minneapolis, MN 55454
(888)672-5437
www.mediafamily.org

Be a Parent, Not a Pushover

This group provides information to parents and other adults about media products and their likely impact on children. Shunning censorship, it seeks to partner parents, organizations, and corporations to create a healthier media diet for families. Its offerings include tips for "taming the tube" (TV), a guide to safe Internet browsing, and ratings of video and computer games.

Center for Media Literacy

3101 Ocean Park Blvd., No. 200
Santa Monica, CA 90405
(800)228-4630
www.medialit.org

Seeking "media literacy education" for all, CML's programs include helping young people acquire "navigational" skills to access information, analyze and explore how media messages (print, verbal, visual, or multimedia) are constructed, and compare and contrast those messages with your own principles.

- Know where they are after school, at night, and on weekends. Demand to know the truth. Require them to eat dinner with the family most nights of the week. Set a time by which they *must* be home at night.
- Find out about their grades. What subjects are they taking and how are they doing? Talk to their teachers and principal, too.
- Make it clear how very, very upset you'd be if they use drugs. Your disapproval could be a strong deterrent.

- Make sure they have assigned chores. Life involves work and responsibility. They might as well get used to it.
- Keep your sense of humor and perspective. Learn to laugh at the little things. Most of your conflicts probably will be relatively small ones, so pick and choose your battles. Don't fret so much about the teen's outside—his or her personal appearance, say, or how he strews clothes around his room. A messy room or outlandish clothes are small potatoes compared to something that may really be harmful, like drugs, cigarettes, or sex.
- Practice listening well. That's the only way you'll develop a real connection with your teen. Follow the listening practices recommended in the previous chapter.
- Learn to communicate well. Talk, don't preach. Conversation, not confrontation. Again, see Chapter 3.
- Teach by example. Mirror the good behavior you seek. And get your spouse on board; standing shoulder to shoulder on your core values sends a good message.

  Especially focus on how you teach your kids to deal with anger. That's one of the most difficult—and most important—tasks of a parent. If your style is angry or confrontational, your kids are unlikely to learn to resolve their conflicts peacefully. If we really want to raise peaceful children, we must learn to be peaceful parents. Teaching a child to deal constructively with conflict is one of the greatest gifts you can give them.
- Stress social responsibility. Encourage your child to "give back" to the community. Encourage him or her to

develop the habit of helping others without reward. Maybe he could cut the grass of the disabled person across the street or do volunteer work for a worthy nonprofit group.

- Be patient. Eventually, they'll mature. The hair will return to something resembling its natural color and the lip ring will come out. Keep reminding yourself that it's better they're rebellious now than 10 or 15 years from now. A rebellious teenager is to be expected; a rebellious 25- or 30-year-old can do some real damage.

Lessons Learned

Your teen needs—and *wants*—your guidance. Give it to them. Don't wimp out on the false belief that he or she might not like you if you spell out some rules. That's probably not true. But even if it were true, what's more important, to be liked but probably not respected by a 16-year-old . . . or have a 16-year-old who has learned valuable life lessons?

So give some guidelines, set some limits. You'll have a better relationship with your teen, especially if you not only talk the talk, but walk the walk. Model the kind of behavior you want the teen to emulate.

And give them praise and affection, whether they ask for it or not. Sometimes we sort of assume that only small kids need lots of attention. And we think that teens, because they lead such active lives, are self-propelled vehicles. They're not. They're just taller versions of the small kids they used to be. And while they may act as if they're above a hug and kudos, teens need acknowledgment as much—and perhaps *more*—than anyone else.

I know it can be frustrating giving love and direction to sometimes rebellious teens who may not seem to respect your efforts. But be kind and generous with your affection. Remember how confusing your teenage years were? How out of touch and irrelevant your parents seemed? How fiercely you desired to be independent?

An old adage from Bible school days still has the ring of truth for me:

If equal love cannot be,
Let the more loving one be me

Yes, I know. Both parents probably work, and time is scarce and you're fatigued. But what are you working for if not to make your family the best it can be? Find the time and make the effort to discover in detail what's going on in your teen's life . . . at school, with friends, and what goes on at home when you're not there.

If all that sounds like a recipe for spending lots more time with your teen, that's because it *is*. For a one-sentence nugget of wisdom about raising teens in general—and specifically for giving them love and direction—it's hard to beat the late Dear Abby's advice:

If you want your children to turn out well, spend twice as much time with them and half as much money.

chapter 5

Step 3: Uniqueness—Knowing What Makes Your Teen Special and Making Sure He/She Knows It, Too

*W*e won't be around forever to protect and nurture our teens. But we can help give them a mastery and self-confidence that will serve them well for the rest of their lives.

Too often, though, bedeviled by our own problems, hampered by shortness of vision, fearful of "spoiling" them, we excel at exhorting them to do better but fail to tell them when they do well. That's not a recipe for creating a well-adjusted adult.

Too many parents assume that their teen *knows* their mother and father are genuinely pleased and proud of them. But I'm convinced from the patients I see—and, in fact, from my own childhood—that that's a dangerous and usually a mistaken assumption.

In this chapter, I want to encourage you to truly appreciate your kid and make a conscious, long-lived effort to bolster him, not tear him down. Doing so can make an impact like few other parental acts.

❧

My mother took great pride in my accomplishments. When I'd get an "A" or get accepted into some club or elected to head the Student Council, her face would light up with incredible incandescence. She would hug me as tightly as if I'd just won the Nobel Prize.

My dad, on the other hand, was slow to praise me or my brothers. The most I seemed to elicit from him when I got good grades or even won a scholarship was a muted "Good Girl." This always bothered me, and so when I was older, I confronted him. Why, I asked, should I continue to work hard and strive, just to receive faint praise or none at all?

He was trying, he said, to encourage humility. "I want you to be beautiful on the inside and not let these things go to your head." My dad said he thought I already had enough confidence, and what I needed was a nudge toward modesty.

Dad's intentions, like those of most parents, were good. It was his execution that was flawed. But little did he realize what an effect his reserve had on me, what a blow he gave for the longest time to my self-esteem.

Are you doing the same to your teen? Are you emotionally stingy because of some vague fear that you'll give him a distorted view of his or her place in the world, that he will act "too big for his britches?"

But ask yourself: *Is that what I'm really afraid of? Or is my real reason for withholding praise that I rarely got any myself?* Hold that thought. We'll come back to that shortly.

Step 3: Uniqueness

What makes your kid unique?

"Unique," according to the dictionary, means the one and only, sole, unequaled, incomparable, and unparalleled. And that *is* your child, a unique collection of traits—never before or since arranged in quite the same order—from your genes and that of your mate.

But our society wars against liking ourselves for who we are. As a people we exalt competition and winning, which means someone has to be a "loser." And our commercial culture ceaselessly taunts us to become something we usually are not—such as beautiful, rich, powerful, and wildly popular.

We must, we're told almost from birth, do better, acquire more, get ahead, though ahead of what we're not quite sure. Day in, day out, in a zillion ways, we're sent the message that we're not yet good enough but maybe we *can* be if we buy a Lexus or a Ford, drink a Coke or a Sprite, smoke a Marlboro or a Camel, clad our feet in Nikes or Adidas, or wear nifty outfits from Banana Republic or The Gap. We live in a world where we judge ourselves and others by the externals.

All this takes its toll as do parents who, often under the weight of their own sense of inferiority, make their kids feel as if they're never quite good enough.

Do you think your kid believes he or she . . .

- has more good traits than bad?
- is essentially lovable?
- can succeed when he or she tries something new?

Do you think your teen has . . .

- pride in who he or she is?

- the ability to tolerate frustration and negative emotions?
- the temperament to act enthusiastically and independently?

We all want children for whom we can answer a resounding "*Yes!*" to those questions. We want our kids to feel terrific about themselves. But many of us as parents don't do what we can when it comes to building a child's positive self-image.

Yet the stakes are high. That sense of how we feel about ourselves, how much we value ourselves, affects how we act toward others and is perhaps *the* major key to a successful life. Children with good self-esteem just have an easier time of it. They do better in school and eventually in jobs. They mesh more easily with classmates, teachers, with parents and other adults in their lives. They view the world as less hostile, more interesting. They're usually healthier, have fewer worries, and are less likely to abuse drugs and alcohol.

And, by contrast, poor self-esteem is among the reasons for failure in school, for lack of occupational aspiration, for a tendency to use and abuse alcohol and drugs, and for many violent behaviors. Even the finest schools and the most sensitive support agencies can't undo the damage of really poor self-esteem.

It's impossible to have *too* much self-esteem. Few, in fact, ever get as much as they need. The worry of parents, like my dad, that too much praise will go to a kid's head and breed arrogance and egotism seems groundless to me. In truth, people with a well-developed sense of self-worth, freed from the fear that they're not good enough, are those who can most afford to be kind and unselfish. Happy with whom they are, they willingly help others.

More than mantras

Yes, improving self-esteem can be the rightful subject of parody if done superficially, insincerely, and reflexively. There's more to improving self-image than mantras about "*I am me and I am enough*" or "*Every day and in every way I am getting better and better.*" Real self-esteem is built on more than just slogans or "feel good" talk.

A truly good self-image is based on evidence, on actions, not just words. But often we—teens especially—need help in pointing out the evidence that exists in the choices that are made, the effort that is exerted, the actions that are taken.

Still, as much as you might wish to, you can't wrap up self-esteem and give it to your kids like a Christmas present. It's a mixture of inborn traits and what happens to them, what they learn about themselves, what they are taught. And who are their primary teachers? The parents, of course. In a broad sense, the ultimate objective of all parenting is to give kids self-esteem.

Self-esteem grows when young people feel valued by those around them, especially by their parents and friends. While you can't do everything, you can do a lot, and toward the end of this chapter I'll suggest specific steps you should consider.

For starters, though, look at yourself. Are you an ultra-controlling parent who gives positive reinforcement only when the teen follows your rigid standards of behavior? Are you still so uptight about your own botched upbringing that you're withholding needed and justified praise? If so, you're damaging your teen.

Of course, you don't set out to do that. You love the kid, right? And you want only the best for him or her? Sure.

But your commitment has to move behind words and beyond vague thoughts. Your mission—if you choose to accept it, as they used to say on that old TV show—is to help your teen become the best person he or she can become. How do you that? In addition to providing food, shelter, and education, you must nurture his or her self-esteem.

Arguably, this is the hardest part of parenting because many adults—perhaps you among them—don't have enough self-esteem of their own. In fact, parents often are woefully deficit. They've been beaten down by their own parents and by life's travails. For many parents, burdened with their owns fears, celebrating their kid's uniqueness is not high on their list of priorities. It's not what they're about. What they're about is just stoically getting by, existing but not really living. For them life is hard, and then you die. And they're none too happy about it all.

If that even remotely describes you, here's your chance to break that mold and leave a lasting legacy: your kid's sense of self-worth. You're not its only determinant, but you have a lot of say. Resolve not to visit upon the son the sins of the father (or mother.) Instead, make it your mission to give your kid the self-esteem he or she needs to have an easier time in life, to get along better with others, to see the world as a place where they are happy and comfortable.

Give them the personal validation that'll stay with them forever. It's probably your most important task as a parent. To grow up feeling good about yourself is a gift for life.

What to do?

Parents can do more than anyone else to promote a child's self-esteem. Your words and actions have an enormous impact. But you must use good judgment and good timing. For example, avoid inflated or inappropriate praise. Children who hear how great they are regardless of their behavior receive conflicting messages. So being overly lenient and passive on the belief that to do otherwise would be to injure the kids' self-esteem is a fool's game.

On the other hand, a kid who is called responsible when he exhibits responsible behavior likely will end up as a responsible adult (providing his parents also model responsible behavior.) In short, we can have a significant impact—though not total control—on who our children become.

Take charge of your own self-esteem, too. Talk aloud about your feelings and the way you cope with problems. For instance, you might say, *This situation at work has been gnawing at me. I'm feeling a little blue. I think I'll take a walk after dinner. Go to the park maybe. Then I'll feel better.* That sends the message that individuals can have some control over how they feel and how they think about themselves.

Don't just tell teens how to live, *show* them. Show your kids how you derive pleasure and satisfaction from refining your character, performing acts of kindness, taking responsibility for yourself, and seeking wisdom and truth. Show them how you support right over wrong. Show them, for instance, by cheering as loudly for the person who visits the nursing home as for the quarterback who throws the winning pass. Shower more kudos on the person who gets control over his emotions than he who fires off a nasty note or makes a sharp verbal thrust. Show them by supporting those who fight for a good, if losing, cause and those who do what's ethical even if at great personal risk. Show them by spending time on activities that have meaning and purpose, that really affect the world and the people in it. Celebrate not just warriors but peacemakers. Make as big a fuss about your kid's acts of lovingkindness as you do about his "A's" in math.

Some other suggestions:

Praise generously but genuinely

Teens aren't mind readers. Don't expect them to *know* when you're feeling good thoughts about them. Make it a point to catch them doing something right, not just something wrong.

This doesn't have to be a big, solemn deal. It can be as simple as just mentioning, *That's a talent I wish I had* or *Gee, you can be proud of that accomplishment* or *That's great. Way to go.* Hugs, smiles, and other warm gestures can help send the message as well.

If giving praise like this doesn't come naturally to you, try keeping a small notebook and writing in it one thing you say each day to convey the message that you think highly of your teen. If you notice that days go by without having anything to write, you'll know you must work harder to make positive

Need a nudge to become more complimentary? Here's a simple, two-step plan:

Step 1: Many different behaviors, some small and seemingly insignificant, make important contributions to relationship satisfaction. List 10 positive things that your teen does that please you.

1. _____
2. _____
3. _____
4. _____
5. _____
6. _____
7. _____
8. _____
9. _____
10. _____

Step 2: Show him or her the list.

daily comments. All children thrive on praise and affection, but it's especially important during the teen years. So believe in and support your teen, even when he or she is being difficult. In fact, *especially* when he or she is being difficult.

But don't praise so freely that you devalue your words of encouragement. And don't append to your kudos a stipulation that he do even better next time. Attach your praise to worthy acts (*Nice going in getting an 'A' in speech class. I could never do that,*) not just *You're a good boy* or *I'm glad you 'aced' speech; now get that math grade up.*

And don't be afraid to praise in front of family or friends; it's that much sweeter when you do.

Help them inventory their strengths

In a quiet moment when you're alone with your teen and he or she is feeling low, be their best friend and help them catalogue their best traits. Talking about their virtues is fine. Even better, write them down together. The ideas stick better that way.

Respect your teens and others

If you want your kids to respect you, themselves, and other adults, show them how. Model respect to them by showing respect to your spouse, to your neighbors, to people different from you. And respect the teens, too—show them that you value their opinions even though you may not always agree with them. Respect their need for space or privacy. Respect their dignity by laughing with them, not at them.

Respect them by apologizing when you do something wrong. And respect them even as you discipline them—by not getting personal, by not hitting or name-calling, by saying, in effect, "Even though I am angry at you, I will not hurt you. I love you."

You want to use well-timed words and actions that, in effect, say: "You are a capable and competent person. Your assets are many."

Step 3: Uniqueness

Avoid using ridicule or shame

Sometimes parents do need to criticize a teen's actions. But insensitive criticism is the quickest way to both weaken a person's self-image and poison a relationship.

Encouragement builds self-esteem, but insensitive criticism tears it down. (Even a single hurtful remark can stay embedded in a young person's consciousness. Can't you still recall some stinging rebuke you got as a teen?)

So it's important to keep such moments on a high plane by using "I" statements rather than "You" statements. For instance, if your daughter fails to clean up the family room as required, you might say *"I think a messy family room makes others feel not so great about their living space"* rather than *"You're so lazy. Don't you ever do what you're supposed to do?"* (See Chapter 3 for more on communicating positively.)

Often the difference between encouragement and criticism is a slight change of tone and a re-wording. For instance:

Criticism: *I knew I couldn't trust you to drive safely. You're just not a careful enough person.*

Encouragement: *Well, the good news is that nobody got hurt. We can fix the fender. But I'm glad you're O.K.*

Criticism: *You call that baked chicken?*

Encouragment: *Thanks for baking the chicken. That saved me a lot of time. Let me show you next time how I do the basting.*

Criticism: *Another "D" in English? What a dummy!*

Be a Parent, Not a Pushover

Encouragement: *Do you think having a better study schedule would help get that English grade up? We could make a rule about having the TV off on school nights. I'd miss some of my shows, but that's O.K. if it helps you out.*

Sure, there may be much to criticize. Maybe you don't like his or her outfits or philosophy or fondness for shrieking music and chaotic closets. But ask yourself: Is what they're doing or saying dangerous to themselves or others, or terribly upsetting to you? If not, maybe you should consider just letting go, abandoning all hopes for perfection. Probably the more you can let go, the better you'll both be.

Avoid pointed comparisons to other kids

Your teen's self-image isn't helped by being compared to his or her siblings, relatives, rivals, or friends. The truth is, your kid *is* incomparable. There's no one else exactly like him nor will there ever be.

When you go to the zoo, you're amazed at the variety of creatures—their sizes, their shapes, and their mission in nature. Be they snakes or birds or bears, they're all part of a plan, and each makes its own contribution. Well, how about the variety of *children*? Don't expect them to all behave the same. And don't nag them to be all the same. Delight in their diversity. Our children are as varied as we are.

Try to understand what's special and different about your kid—and then honor that. Each child is a complex human being. And though your teens are of you, they are *not* you. Nor are they just like their brothers or sisters.

Step 3: Uniqueness

Sometimes perplexed parents ask, "How could these children brought up by the same parents in the same house be so different?" Well, they *weren't* brought up by the same parents in the same house. Each child is raised by what amounts to a different set of parents and in a different home: The first-born, for example, is at least for a time an only child of highly inexperienced parents with what probably are too-lofty expectations. Younger siblings, on the other hand, are nurtured by more seasoned parents. These later arrivals have brothers and sisters, too, and must adapt to a different world, including less physical space and more sharing.

Don't compare your kid to you . . . or the mythical you.

Raising children is not a chance to relive your own life or make up for your own lost opportunities. You can't step into the same river twice, as the old saying goes. Not only are their genes different, but their environment is different from the one you faced. So your kids are unlikely to fit the mold you have in mind.

One father I know tried zealously to get his oldest son to capture the athletic glories that had eluded the dad. From an early age, the boy was encouraged—pushed, even—to get into football, soccer, tennis, baseball, swimming, you name it. However, the son wasn't very good or interested in sports.

The defining moment came when the boy, a reluctant goalie in soccer, was so intrigued by the patterns in the chalk forming the box around the goal that he failed to even look up as an opponent's incoming shot soared past him for the winning point. That was the last straw!

Be a Parent, Not a Pushover

The father thereafter gave up trying to make the son a sports hero. Instead, he surrendered to the boy's uniqueness and gave free rein to the kid's tendencies toward art and beauty. The son since has become an accomplished teenage actor, with starring roles in a number of local plays and musicals. And the dad now brags of the son's "Redford-like electricity" with the same passion he might earlier have reserved for a two-run double to left field.

Encourage positive self-talk

We all chatter, inwardly or outwardly, to ourselves, but teens often adopt a negative self-talk that may be a sign of anxiety or depression. It's talk—but it's also more than that. Because what they say may show what they're thinking and that may affect how they feel and behave.

So if you catch your kid saying *Our team can't win for losing* or *I can't ever get any credit for all the good work I do at school*, gently redirect him or her. Perhaps with a smile, you might encourage him to say something more along the lines of *Our team gave it our best shot. Some days you're the bug, some days you're the windshield.* Or *It feels good to do good, even if no one appears to notice at first. But eventually they will. They always do.*

Instill self-discipline

People who have discipline, who understand the payoff for delaying gratification, have happier, more fulfilling lives. (See Chapter 4 for thoughts on how to give the proper direction to your teen.)

Teens need to accept responsibility for their behavior. They need to learn that actions have consequences, and good actions usually have good consequences. You're the main teacher. In a fair, firm, and friendly way you can create the rules—and enforce the discipline if the rules are broken.

Intellectual ability alone is not enough for success. As Dr. Daniel Goleman pointed out in his best-selling book *Emotional Intelligence: Why It Can Matter More Than IQ*, how we handle our emotions—including how readily we delay gratification to reach a specific goal—and how we recognize emotions in others counts for so much more in having a successful life than do SAT scores or graduate degrees.

Promote good decision making

Having the confidence to make good decisions is a major component of self worth. Any teen who is making consistently bad choices, such as engaging in self-destructive behavior, will not be helped by being told, *"Feel better about yourself. You have intrinsic self-worth."* He or she will not improve their self-image until better choices start being made.

So ask the teen to pinpoint the problem that's behind any needed change. Brainstorm with him the possible solutions; in all likelihood, you'll come up with some that he has overlooked. Walk him through the consequences of each, but allow him to choose among them.

Later, you can help him evaluate how it worked out. Once he gets the hang of it, his ability to make good decisions—and his self-esteem—will improve. You want him or her to know they can work out problems if they stick with them. And to know that a problem in one part of their lives doesn't mean their whole life is in tatters.

So encourage your teen to make more of his or her own decisions. That shows them they are trusted. Don't rush in to rescue him from every frustrating experience. Instead, encourage him to solve the problem independently. If needed, help him come up with alternatives, but let him choose among them. Challenge them with the freedom, the opportunity, to make choices.

Temper assertiveness with reason

Encourage your kids to speak up, to ask for what they want, but to realize there's no reason they must get it and certainly no logic in being angry if they don't. You want them not to be shy in asking for something, but not to feel entitled to it, either. As in all things teachable, set a good example as well.

Discourage the blame game

Make it clear that they are ultimately responsible for any feeling they experience. Similarly, they are not responsible for how others feel. Most of all, avoid blaming them for how *you* feel. When a parent says *"You drive me crazy,"* that makes more of a statement about the adult than about the teen, but he or she is going to interpret the remark—especially if it's repeated—as a harsh put-down.

Help de-emphasize physical beauty

Sure, it's nice to be good looking. But we all know good-looking people who are jerks or who are unhappy with themselves. Our culture puts much emphasis on looks, especially for girls. But parents don't need to reinforce that.

Promote a sense of security by avoiding chaos and fighting at home

Nothing undercuts a young person's sense of being wanted and loved as much as parents who are yelling and carrying on. That makes what should be a sanctuary into a scary place. Kids, no matter what their age, will recoil or rebel. A stable family environment is in everyone's best interests.

Develop connectedness

Everybody needs linkages to life, and the more teens have, the better they will feel about themselves, whether the activity is raising goldfish or belonging to an "in" social club. There is a direct correlation between self-esteem and the number of things about life with which we're fully engaged.

A wide range of hobbies and interests will give the teen a chance to do something special, to be part of a group, to feel connected, to develop significant relationships, and to be affirmed by others.

Foster social consciousness

Another avenue to teen self-worth is getting them involved in something larger than themselves. Tutoring friends, baking cookies for a newcomer in the neighborhood, babysitting for free for a needy family, stuffing envelopes for a worthy fund-raiser, all such activities teach our kids to rise above their own wants and needs. Acts of kindness, even if they stem from a desire to feel better about ourselves, help us internalize the trait of compassion.

Assist development of spirituality

Spirituality means an attachment or sensitivity to religious and/or moral values. Spirituality comes in many stripes; it doesn't merely require going to church or professing some orthodox belief.

A variety of studies have found that religious belief and practice is associated with less risk of self-destructive behaviors (such as suicide, smoking, drug and alcohol abuse), less perceived stress, and greater life satisfaction among adults and youth.

How do you foster spirituality in personal and family life? Some ideas:

- *A first step is to examine your central values.* And, more important, how well you live by them? Ask yourself, what's most important to me? How do my daily actions mirror those values? Then take steps to narrow the gap between what you say you believe and what you do. If, for instance, you say family is foremost but you spend practically every waking hour at work, that should tell you something. Your teen is probably quicker to pick up on this anomaly than you are.
- *Make time each day for prayer or meditation.* Plus, encourage your family to do the same. This is not something you can decree; you'll need to demonstrate. Taking time to read from the Bible can be a rich source of inspiration. The Psalms speak to everyone.

Perhaps you'll want to combine this with the reading of inspirational literature or by use of relaxation techniques, such as deep breathing or visualization.

- *Experience nature.* Even if you just take a walk along the creek or spend a few minutes staring into a star-filled sky, you can marvel at the wonders of the universe—and silently show your teen there's more to life than MTV and video games. You might start doing these things by yourself at first, then extend an invitation to your kid if he or she shows an interest.

Laugh with your teens . . . and encourage them to laugh at themselves

Especially during times of tension, humor is an effective means of communication. People who take themselves too seriously miss a lot that life has to offer.

Lessons Learned

No one feels good about himself or herself all the time. And positive self-esteem doesn't happen overnight; in fact, true self-worth is developed over a lifetime.

But if you put some of these principles into practice, your teen is likely to feel better *more* of the time. You'll be giving him or her a head start on having a better self-image.

Take delight in your kid, and that delight will fuel his or her self-esteem. Because, in truth, teens are gluttons for praise. Feed that hunger—but feed it honestly. Insincere or superficial praise is probably worse than none at all; it just teaches the teen to doubt your every utterance.

Be a Parent, Not a Pushover

Strive to be more of a coach than, say, a cheerleader. A coach uses praise to foster growth and instill self-worth; a cheerleader just throws hoorays out to the universe.

Love and respect your kid, and the benefits will multiply. As they see how careful you are with their sensitive souls, they will learn to also be careful with themselves and others.

A good parent helps his kids develop a roadmap to their own unique personalities. To do that, you've got to really *know* your child. Teens need for us to be involved in their lives. There's no way around it—that means spending a lot of time with the teen. If you don't, you'll give them further reason to question your sincerity.

Avoid comparing the performances of your kid with others or with you as a youngster. Work to help your kids feel good about themselves because they are doing the things they are created to do, things that have meaning and purpose, things that really affect the world and its people.

Learn to accept your teens for who they are. Maybe your kid is not the perfect human being. If he or she doesn't live up to your dreams, then perhaps you need to re-adjust your dream to fit reality. So he's not the most cerebral kid you've ever seen. Or the tidiest or the most punctual or the most diligent. But, on the other hand, is he perhaps easygoing and fun to be around? That's excellent, too.

Or maybe with his tin ear, he isn't going to be the classical pianist you hoped, but with his organizing skills he could be a great manager. Or quite possibly he's none of those, and instead is just a warm and generous human being who may not do great things but will do small things with great love.

Step 3: Uniqueness

A garden is an apt metaphor for life in so many ways, not the least of which is raising your kids. In your flower garden, you plant seeds, nurture them, and try to protect, let's say, your marigolds from pests, from frost, from storms. If you do all this and you're patient, you end up with a healthy marigold plant with lovely yellow or orange blossoms. But no matter how hard you try, you won't be able to turn that marigold into a rose or a lily.

Each child is a unique flower, too, one that's never before blossomed. Nurture that flower. Feed it, protect it, study and learn from it even as you look for its unique bloom. That bloom can't be hurried. It's got to spring forth at its own pace and in its own way. And when it finally does, that blossom may not be precisely the color or shape you saw in your dreams . . . but it is the way it was meant to be.

chapter 6

Step 4:
Love, or the
Magic of Real

We'd all agree that love is the most powerful of human emotions. But it's also the most complicated. And never more so than with our children who, of course, both delight and bedevil us.

I know you really love your children. But your concept of love probably implies dependence: You may love them in part because they are dependent on you . . . and in a sense, you are dependent on them. They depend on you for food, shelter, and nurturing. You depend on them for a sense of being truly connected to life. They are your umbilical cord to all of creation, your tie to the passage of time.

The Lebanese poet Kahlil Gibran spoke passionately and clearly about this shade of parental love in *The Prophet* when he wrote, "Your children are not your children. They are the sons and daughters of Life's longing for itself."

It's been said that you can only give your children two things: roots and wings. But when the wings start to sprout, the dance between love and dependence can get difficult.

Be a Parent, Not a Pushover

When the child moves toward *in*dependence, the relationship that both parties have gotten so used to may really start to unravel. Both parent and child may begin to doubt the authenticity, the realness, of the other's love.

And, of course, moving toward independence is what the teen years are all about. Slowly and unevenly, teens begin to let go of their roots and go aloft with their new-found wings. That's scary to them—and usually to us.

In this chapter I want to explore the nature of parental love and point you in the direction of some ways to try to make your love more genuine, more real, and more enduring for your teen.

The curse of conditionality

The challenge is to love unconditionally. That is a big order. It means loving others for their worth as human beings, loving them despite faults, bad moods, and the way they leave peanut butter smudges on the kitchen counter or crumpled fenders on the family car.

Many parents tend to withhold their love when their teens are not behaving as adults believe they should. That's conditional love, based on your idea of good behavior, and it's not very effective. It sends the message that you love them for what they do for you (act politely, get good grades, make the varsity, etc.) rather than for who they are.

Of course, we all want our kids to do well and succeed. But if we're really honest with ourselves, we probably recognize we want this for two reasons: (1) so they'll thrive and have a good life; and (2) so their success will make us appear as good parents. Not necessarily in that order, either.

If your teen screws up, do you interpret that as evidence that you're a poor parent? When he or she performs well, or poorly, in front of others, does it appear to you as if others are scrutinizing you? For many of us it does. And likely we withdraw emotionally from the poor-performing teen, who will feel rejected even if we try to put on a good face.

It's important, though, for our sake and for our kids' sakes, that we seek to lessen this guilt /pride by association. We should want our kids to have a good life because we love them, period. Not because it will make us seem to be superior parents.

If you're inclined to see your child's success or failure as reflective of your competence as a parent, maybe you need to rethink your sensitivity to what others think, rethink that underlying premise. You may be mistaken to believe that when your child receives praise (or criticism) from your peers it means you are more accepted (or rejected.)

Even if you are right, even if many people are so narrow-minded as to make lasting, critical judgments of a parent based on the child's behavior, should you *care*? Ask yourself, what's more important: Looking good to the Joneses down the street, or helping your teen develop into the best person he or she can become? If the Joneses think less of you because your boy got caught drinking with some of his underage buddies, so be it. If he didn't hurt himself or anyone else, what's it to the Joneses? You know your boy has many good attributes that aren't erased by a few illicit beers on a Saturday night. It may actually turn out to be a growth experience for him.

Be a Parent, Not a Pushover

Too often, though, we become conditional parents who love our kids when they reflect well on us and disdain them when they don't. It isn't enough that they be good; they must be ideal. In myriad ways we make this clear to them, too. Idealization sometimes can serve a person well in many areas of life, including parenting. But it also can cause trouble when it gets the best of you.

Not a rationale for indifference

Your thoughts and feelings greatly affect your action. If your kid screws up, you probably withdraw emotionally, if only for a brief time. Even if you offer tepid words of encouragement (*You did O.K., son*), a sensitive child will feel your withdrawal and will likely interpret it as rejection anyhow.

Parents too often use love and approval as a payoff for excellent performance. If you hold back emotionally when your teen fails and hug him or her enthusiastically only when he triumphs, he will learn to associate good performance with love and poor performance with rejection. So you may need to watch your reactions.

Be there when they're down, too. Be there when they fail to make the football team, forget their lines in the play, or have a miserable date. At such times, spare them the lecture; just show your love.

Don't get me wrong, I'm not saying punishing or disapproving of a teen's action is wrong. In fact, a theme of this book is that you *must* set limits, you must draw boundaries and act if those boundaries are violated. But what I am saying is when your rejection of performance is woven into your reactions, when your message about the kid's worth and the kid's performance get blended, that's dangerous. That's conditional love. And it can mess up a kid.

Truth is, children usually come to see themselves as their parents see them. And if we love them only when it's convenient, only when they're successful and we can bask in that success, we may be creating future adults who will polish the pebbles of superficial success and diminish the diamonds of true self-worth.

Seeking detachment

I have had many parents (especially men) say that they do not believe that unconditional love exists. They ask, *So how can I possibly show love for my kid when he/she has pushed every button I have?*

The answer: detachment, or what's sometimes called non-attachment. Parents must detach in order to help their teens become autonomous. Note that I said detachment, *not* disconnection. There's a difference. Detachment is a skill that takes a lot of practice, but I guarantee you'll get a positive payoff.

Detachment means *staying in the relationship, but remaining loose.* It means keeping a bit of a psychological distance. It means seeing yourself as an *observer* rather than someone who's elated or wounded by your teen's every minor triumph or small misstep.

How do you do that? By getting out of the habit of taking everything personally, by refusing to see the relationship as a zero-sum game in which one or the other of you is always scoring points or being scored upon. Your relationship with your kid shouldn't be like an athletic contest with offense and defense, winners and losers, and a final score.

A better metaphor might be a symphony: a long-playing work that is at times upbeat, but at other points contemplative, or even dark and foreboding but always changing, adapting. The symphonic components respond to one another, but they don't compete. And the end result? A feeling, a statement, a sensibility—but not a winner and a loser. A symphony is a creative work, not a contest for cumulative points.

In any of life's arenas, truly successful people are those who are able to detach from unsuccessful and undesirable past events. This does not mean that they forget their mistakes, only that they are able to step back from them and grow.

Detachment allows parents to recognize and dismantle blame, eliminate any controlling response, and allow their teen to take responsibility for his or her actions. Parents must examine their own lust for control that could be robbing the teen of taking responsibility for his or her own actions.

I have had this conversation about detachment many times with my daughter and her response is usually, *It sounds like you disconnect from the person and doesn't than mean that you stop loving them?* Quite the contrary!

You love them just as much. But you love them as an observer and a helper, not an embattled participant whose own sense of self-worth soars or plummets on the outcome of every new development in their young life.

A friend of mine tells of visiting a couple who were lighthouse keepers on a remote rock off the coast of British

Columbia. The pair had spent their whole adult life tending to lighthouses and had raised their kids there, though the now-grown children lived more conventional lives on the mainland. Once a month the parents received mail by helicopter.

Someone asked the mother if that wasn't difficult to hear from her kids and grandkids only once every 30 days. "Oh, no. It's wonderful," she said, with a chuckle. "That's because I know that whatever crisis they're describing in their letter has been solved by the time I read it."

In that case, geography created the detachment. But there's probably a lesson for us all in there. Time marches on. Crises ebb and flow and in retrospect probably weren't such big deals after all.

This, too, shall pass

This detachment is what it takes to truly love unconditionally. But how do you stay cool and remain moderate when your teen is acting so heatedly, so immoderately?

For starters, begin to observe your reactions to your teen's actions. Remind yourself not to get upset because your daughter didn't tidy up her room as you asked her. Ask her again, but keep in mind the kid is just that, a kid. Further, note that you're not a failure as a parent if socks and underwear are strewn wildly around her bedroom. The sock and underwear police aren't going to take you away. Your name isn't going to be posted on the community bulletin board as "Inept Housekeeper." This, too, shall pass.

Secondly, keep in mind that we're all amalgams of virtues and vices, strengths and weaknesses. And what you focus on is what you'll get more of. Yes, ask again that she clean up her room. But even as you do so, concentrate on her positive attributes. That'll help put her untidiness in perspective.

Thirdly, make an effort to not just love your teen when he or she is being good. Love him when he's being bad, too. The message you want to send—to yourself and to him—is: I will love you no matter what.

Like true north or the perfect wave

Unconditional love requires unconditional praise. But too often the message we send isn't that clear and simple. Instead it's a mixed bag that confuses more than buoys.

How? By directly or indirectly communicating that our kids' performances aren't good enough. For example, as Monica Ramirez Basco in *Never Good Enough* points out, we too often send mixed messages in which we praise and criticize simultaneously, such as *That was a good* ____ (catch/recital/play/report card, etc.) *but I bet you can do better.*

Also, as I mentioned, when our children make mistakes or perform below our standards, many parents respond by showing disapproval and withdrawing their affections. The message is *Get it right and I will approve of you.* Over time this conditionality may become internalized so that the child demands constant perfection from himself, which is a recipe for a life of frustration.

Unconditional love means loving your teen no matter what he looks like, no matter how she acts, and no matter how well he performs. That doesn't mean you always like how she looks, acts, or performs.

Emotionally, teenagers are still children. And they will sometimes act like it. Thus, their behavior may be unpleasant. But if you only love your teenager conditionally—that is, when he pleases you—and if you only convey your love during those times, he or she won't feel genuinely loved. What happens then? The teen will feel insecure and incompetent. He will believe it's fruitless to do his best because that is never enough. Insecurity, anxiety, and low self-esteem probably will bedevil him. And that may prevent him from developing more mature behavior. So, in short, parents are partially responsible for a teen's behavioral development.

On the other hand, if you love a teenager without conditions, he or she likely will feel good about himself and comfortable with himself. He'll be able to control his anxiety and thus, he'll be able to control his behavior.

Without unconditional love, parenting can be a confusing and frustrating burden. But when you begin with unconditional love, you can fulfill your teen's needs *and* feel good about yourself as a parent.

Unconditional love is an ideal, like true north or the perfect wave. Perhaps it is impossible to feel unconditional love for anyone 100% of the time. But the closer you can approach this goal, the better both of you will feel and the stronger your relationship will be.

The source of power

The strength of your love is going to be a key to every facet of that relationship. You may think you have "power" over your kid because you're the parent. And maybe you did when he or she was small.

But in the adolescent years, brute strength and intimidation no longer work. The only real and lasting parental power with a teenager flows from the influence of love. If a teen has gotten love from you, he or she will return it. If he cares about his parents, he'll try to do the right thing when faced with a temptation. If he doesn't care about them, he'll do what he wants to, or maybe yield to the temptation just to spite them.

Over a long period of time you have the opportunity to build this love into the cornerstone of your relationship. How? By not just talking about love but by showing it. The more positive attention you give your child, the more loving he or she will become. Yet research indicates that the average parent gives his or her child approximately 96% negative attention—instructions, threats, punishments, sarcasm, and so on—and only 4% positive.

Of course, it's impossible to be a good parent without giving a child, especially a small child, negative attention. But the issue becomes one of degree. If the parent predominantly takes positive actions (such as giving praise, listening non-judgmentally, relaxing with the kid or working together side by side), the child will get the message that he is loved. And that's the most important message of all.

On getting real

Do you remember the classic children's book by Margery Williams, *The Velveteen Rabbit?* It was one of my kids' favorites. The story goes like this: A young boy discovers a beautiful velveteen rabbit in his Christmas stocking. He plays with it for a while, then casts it aside. The stuffed bunny ends up in the closet, where it is snubbed by the more expensive mechanical toys. But the rabbit eventually learns from another old toy, the Skin Horse, an important lesson about how to become real.

What is real, the rabbit asks, thinking of the fancier mechanical toys. "Does it mean having things that buzz inside you and a stick-out handle?"

"Real isn't how you are made," replies the Skin Horse. "It's a thing that happens to you. When a child loves you for a long, long time, not just to play with but *really* loves you, then you become Real."

The Skin Horse explains that when you're Real, sometimes it hurts but you don't mind. And becoming Real takes a long time. "But these things don't matter at all, because once you are Real you can't be ugly, except to people who don't understand."[*]

From then on, the little rabbit yearns for nothing so much as to be Real—and of course, eventually the rabbit becomes real, with the help of the magic fairy.

But, of course, like most children's stories, this one has a deeper meaning. It's about the long-term payoff of loving unconditionally. The little boy came to love the rabbit. "To him he was always beautiful, and that was all that the little Rabbit cared about. He didn't mind how he looked to other people, because the nursery magic had made him Real, and when you are Real shabbiness doesn't matter."

And when you love unconditionally, of course, achievement and other people's assessments don't matter.

---

[*] Quoted with permission from *The Velveteen Rabbit* by Margery Williams. Published by Henry Holt and Company, New York, 1983.

Be a Parent, Not a Pushover

I read that story again and again to my kids. They, now grown, and I have talked often about being Real. Not long ago, I put the question to them: *What made you feel real?*

One, now in her early 30s and with children of her own, wrote "My mother. No, I'm not just saying that. She has always taught me to be a compassionate and loving person. She has always accepted me for who I was and would let me make my own mistakes but she stayed by my side to pick me up and support me and love me for who I am."

She also cited her faith and the unconditional love she gets from her family. "My husband and kids remind me exactly how 'real' I am every day. I can make mistakes but that is human and I am still a good mom and wife. I don't have to pretend that I'm something I'm not."

A step-daughter, also in her 30s and married, wrote, "At the end of the day, no matter how great I handled this person or that situation at work or at home, or how horribly I failed, I still go to sleep next to my partner in life and know that he still thinks I'm beautiful. That's *real*."

Mapping a plan of action

Stay detached. Stay cool. Work at loving unconditionally. Encourage mature behavior. This all sounds good, but how, exactly do you do it?

Some suggestions:

Express love and acceptance separately

Don't make acceptance of the teen conditional upon good performance. Praise the action when the kid does something you like (*"Nice job washing the car."*) but keep expressions (*"You're such a wonderful kid!"*) of love and acceptance separate and try not to mix the two, as you might if you said, *"Thanks for washing the car. You're such a terrific boy! I love you very much."* Conversely, don't criticize the child (*"You're lazy and always have been!"*) instead of criticizing the behavior (failing to wash the car.) When you need to scold or condemn, make the criticism about the action, not about the kid's worth. It's wonderful to express love all the time ... but not just as a reward for superior performance.

Get over the idea that you're being judged by your teen's achievements

Don't take it so personally. We're each—child and parent—responsible for our actions. You're not a bad parent if your kid does poorly in one thing, or even several things. Try to transcend your own self-consciousness. When a child has a problem, it's not necessarily about you.

Support and acknowledge your teens when they've done poorly, too

Don't hold back affection, or threaten to do so, because of poor performance. If anything, that's when the teen needs it most. *I love you and admire you*, you might say, or *I think you're a terrific person.*

Don't mix praise with imperatives to improve

Avoid mixed messages of praise and improvement, such as *That was fine* , but . . . . If you do, the teen will hear the criticism that follows the "but" and will deduce that the "fine" was insincere. Save the improvement lecture for another time.

Don't use threats to promote performance

If you say *You better get a good grade—or else!* or *You'll be grounded for a week if you don't play up to your potential,* you're expressing love conditionally and in the starkest terms.

Don't criticize them in front of others

Even in the Army, hardly a place for sensitive souls, there's a rule: Praise in public, criticize in private. That's a good one for parents, too.

Don't hide your mistakes or weaknesses from your kids

If you do, they won't have a very realistic view of life—or of you. Much of what kids learn is through example. And if you try to display flawlessness, well, that's not very realistic. Instead reveal your errors and how you cope, including how you accept responsibility. The message: Yes, you sometimes screw up, too, but the world doesn't come to an end, and neither you nor I is a lesser person for making a mistake.

Encourage them to set their own goals rather than blindly adopt yours

That's what they're going to need to do as adults, so you might as well start helping them now. Instead of you telling them "*I expect all 'A's next semester,*" have a dialogue.

As a general rule, questions work far better than orders or ultimatums. For instance:

> *How do you feel about last semester's grades?*
> *How would you go about raising them?*
> *How many 'A's can you realistically expect next semester?*
> *How can I help you reach that goal?*
> *What would it take to increase that number? Fewer classes?*
> *Less TV? A new computer?*

The point is to make him or her *want* to put in the effort rather than be pushed to do so because he feels *"If I don't make this GPA, my parents are going to kill me."*

Lessons Learned

Love your kids unconditionally. Tell them you have confidence in them, that you will care for them no matter what they accomplish. Deliver that message consistently and *mean* it when you say it. Kids are very good at detecting inconsistency and insincerity.

Be slow to anger and quick to forgive. Support achievement but try to avoid making it a pawn in some power struggle between you and your kid.

Don't stint on spending time with them. Staying connected with them during their teenage years is probably the best inoculation that they'll receive for protection from life's tougher travails. Giving that love won't guarantee they'll turn out just the way you want them to or that they'll be spared difficulty. But your love greatly increases the odds that despite the difficulties, they will become fully functioning adults, and become a son or daughter you will be proud of.

And be kind. Remember that everyone wants to do well . . . but everyone is fighting a difficult battle.

chapter 7

Step 5: Teaching—Sharing What You Believe

At the close of the Christmas meal, when stomachs are full and joy is abundant, a mother I know passes out the dessert plates around the large table. Then she sits down, takes a deep breath, and looks lovingly at her family. Some of her seven children and step-children look away in a futile attempt to stifle snickers. Others watch Mom, their eyes dancing with expectation, their lips already beginning to curl in a smile.

"It's that time of year . . . " she begins—and then the air is instantly filled with jeers and flying dinner rolls!

Mom—and I must confess, that's *me*—is about to give what's become lovingly known in our family as "The Talk," a ritual that is as sappy as it is beloved. Typically, I give a little speech and then pose the question, *"How have you served and given back this year?"* Everyone takes a turn at answering.

The whole process takes maybe half an hour out of an entire year. But it looms large in our family. We've been doing it for decades. In fact, it's evolved into a tradition that is one of the things holding us together, helping to make our family *a family.*

As the children have gotten older and even had children of their own, they playfully boo and make fun of my rite. And one year I remember thinking maybe we'd outgrown this ritual. So I decided to skip it.

Big mistake! The kids soon took up the call, "Com'on, Mom, where's 'The Talk'?" And I realized that despite the jests, this little ceremony had become meaningful.

Yes, it's a target for mild ridicule, but it's also a deeply-ingrained practice that we have come to need as a sailor needs a compass.

❦

A family ritual is a special way of doing things that's full of meaning and is repeated over and over. Rituals show our beliefs and values in action and create a sense of belonging. They're one of the best things we can do to help our kids—and maybe ourselves—navigate through major life changes.

Taken together, these ceremonies give, at the least, something of a signature to a family and, at best, they weave a web of life that can support our teens in troubled times. Rituals are especially good for families that are blended through divorce and remarriage and thus, perhaps more than most, need a glue to bind them.

Many times the importance of ritual shows up in later years. When the children grow up and live away from home, the "weird" rituals that Mom and Dad used to insist on take on added meaning, sometimes culminating in the demand for an encore. Over time, we all learn the unspoken message of rituals: The family is important and will be there for us, no matter what.

Rituals are a form of teaching that's greatly underrated and rarely discussed. Yet every family needs special days, celebrations, and ceremonies to help its members slow down and savor life. So in this chapter I want to talk about how positive rituals can send the right messages to your teens . . . and give you some ideas about rituals you might want to create.

How do we teach?

What do I mean by *teaching*? In this case I don't mean classrooms, books, or trips to the library or the Internet. I mean giving our children connections that may prevent them from losing their way. Rituals are like signposts that say, *Family →* *This way* or *← What we believe in, 1 mile.*

In real life, of course, signposts don't absolutely ensure you won't get lost. And they certainly don't take the trip for you. But they're a big help in aiding the traveler in finding out where he or she is in relation to the destination.

Family rituals work the same way. They help the alert family member keep his or her bearings. And they provide an opportunity for repetition so that the family's values can be driven home.

Lessons in behavior

Albert Schweitzer, the great scientist and humanitarian, once listed three important ways in which we teach our youngsters: "The first is by example. The second is by example. The third is by example." Indeed, *showing* your kids how to be a good person—rather than just telling them to be—is a recurring theme of this book.

We impact our kids greatly because, whether we know it or they know it, we as adults are *always* role modeling. How Aunt Hope treats Uncle Jim, how grown-up males and females act around one another, how parents relax at the Labor Day picnic where there's plenty of beer and foolishness, how they interact when watching or playing sports, what they say in private about people of other nationalities, races, or religions—these are all opportunities for teaching and learning.

So, you have many chances to give subtle lessons in behavior. You're giving one every moment you're with your teen. You're always on display; the teen is always picking up on your behavior through osmosis. Don't flub it.

But rituals are a different, more conscious way of teaching by example. And all societies and families have them. In fact, teens are awash in societal rituals. There's the high school prom. Pep rallies. Getting a driver's license. The first date. Graduation. Maybe choosing a college. All these are supposed to mark the passage into adulthood and inculcate certain values, such as responsibility, social acumen, and preparing for one's life work.

And all families have their own routines, certain ways of repeatedly doing things that become part of the domestic fabric and are done largely without thinking. Part of this is history born of preferences. For example, where we each sit at the dinner table, what kind of food is served, and how we conduct ourselves while eating. We usually don't think much about these until, say, we have guests. Then we usually instruct them gently, briefly on the rules, such as *Dad always sits there on the end* or *We always put the salad dressing on the side so people can decide how much they want.*

Other small, almost-automatic rituals can be as tiny as who, by tradition, gets to read which section of the Sunday paper first. Or what is our style when we decorate the Christmas tree—Do we toss the thin silvery icicles in bunches like confetti? Or do we place them carefully strand by strand?

But then some unspoken, un-debated rituals aren't very uplifting. Watching TV for six hours every night, night after night and year after year, until all the family has dozed off is a ritual of sorts. So is making a habit of never being more than a few feet from an open bottle of liquor. Neither of those is likely to be of much help to a teen trying to find his way in the world, unless, of course, he or she is so turned off by those kinds of values that he charts a new, independent course.

Stating your values

But what I want to urge you to think about are the more elaborate rituals that we consciously use to draw the boundaries between our family and the outside world, rituals that silently shout who we are and what we stand for. These can represent our basic values, such as trust, openness, and honesty. Most often, these rituals entail how we relate to one another, how we change, heal, and celebrate.

When I was small, my parents, for example, used to take some time at the first of every year and ask us kids what area of our life we'd like to see change during the next 12 months. Collectively, we would sit and talk about this. Some of us wanted to add new friends, others had athletic aspirations, and still others just wanted less school and more recess.

But as we matured, our would-be changes grew less obvious and more sophisticated. We wanted to be better people, not just accomplish more goals. We desired to be truly honest, perhaps, or better able to give and receive love. To this day, I never rip the "December" off the calendar and stare at a fresh January that I don't think for more than a few moments about what I'd like to do with the 12-month opportunity that beckons.

I've done this ritual with my kids, too. And they seemed to get into in. When I told them the areas of my life where I was seeking improvement, they *really* liked that part. Kids like their parents to own up to their shortcomings; it makes them more real.

For those—like teens—who need substantial support, developing positive rituals should be a priority. Done properly, rituals will help people through major life changes as well as through daily existence.

Repetition is a key element of rituals or traditions and is a great learning tool. So if you decide on a ritual, don't just do it once or twice and let it lapse. Keep at it. Stay on the schedule.

For example, a ritual that I'd recommend is a family meeting, say once a month, to set or repeat the family rules and settle disputes. A family meeting is a great time to expound on the rules, whether it's how much time any one person can have in the bathroom to who's responsible for walking and feeding the dog.

A family council may sound like a quaint idea that went out with armchair doilies, but it can make your home function better. It's especially important for large and/or blended families.

Such a meeting helps families get organized. It showcases the value of cooperation and teamwork. It reminds us to subordinate our individual desires to the common good. Plus, the structure takes a lot of the steam out of disagreements; participants are less likely to yell at one another when in a group discussion.

In fact, you might even want to use the ritual of the family meeting to discuss the family's other rituals. Take an inventory among yourselves. Ask: *What do we do together, over and over, that has special meaning for us?* or *What do we do or say that makes our family different from others?* And *When did we start doing that?* or *Why is that ritual important to us?* Such an inventory might make it easier to begin some new rituals or improve old ones.

You don't want your meeting to be over-complicated by rules, but neither do you want it to become just a gripe fest, with nothing really getting done. So strive for a middle ground between bureaucracy and anarchy. How? Here are some suggestions:

- Meet at a regular time.
- Make a list of topics or an agenda, perhaps posting it earlier on the refrigerator door so others can add to it.
- Take turns being the leader.
- Ask for comments from everyone.
- And focus on actions to be taken, not just complaints to be heard.

Be a Parent, Not a Pushover

The challenge of blended families

Marriages sometimes end, but families do not. Although you may cease being a spouse, you'll be a parent for the rest of your life. And you may end up being a step-parent, too. And that's when the challenges really begin.

At best, the kids feel divided loyalties when a parent divorces and remarries, and at worst, the step-family dissolves into armed camps. If you're old enough to remember the old TV shows *The Brady Bunch* and *Eight is Enough,* you saw large step-families merge seamlessly into cozy, comfortable lives with occasional dilemmas but mostly with fun and games. Were it only true! Actually, while half of all marriages end in divorce, two-thirds of all second marriages do.

It's common in a step-family or a "blended" family, as it's sometimes called when one or both partners bring children from a previous relationship, for youngsters to see the step-parent as an intruder, a blight on the memory of their departed mother or father. Thus, it's hard for them to welcome the adult newcomer.

In fact, the kid may try to move into the void left by the departing parent and act as an equal. Or, the teens also may seek to exploit conflicts to gain advantage over their siblings or stepsiblings. And, naturally, the biological parent has a longer parent/child relationship than he or she does with the new spouse. This often makes the incoming parent feel like an outsider.

If you find yourself in a blended family, remember that it's even harder for the teen than it is for you. Even though he or she is a part of this "new" family, his or her sense of stability has been shattered. Consciously or not, he balks at suggestions that the new family receive his full attention and loyalty.

Thus, "blended" is a hopeful term; more accurately, perhaps, the two families are "mixed" but not really blended. What to do? Research shows that it's important that a child be given permission by the parent and/or step-parent to love the other biological parent. And conversely, he needs to be given permission by the biological parents to like the step-parent. Otherwise, the children are put in a no-win situation.

For two-home families, it's important to develop a working, civil relationship where all the parents and step-parents can communicate and control their feelings. It's especially crucial that children not be used as messengers (*Tell your father he's too cheap; I need more money*) between households or as pawns (*You've got to spend Christmas Day with us, no matter what*) in a power struggle.

What's this mean for rituals? Blending two families is a lot like merging two businesses. Such a merger would never happen without team meetings and discussions of goals.

Blended families essentially start from scratch in developing cohesiveness. Children of divorce yearn even more than most for structure and consistency. So rituals become doubly important. So here are some ideas to keep in mind as you try to "blend" the new family:

- Re-tooling old rituals with a new cast may just create nostalgia for an era that's not returning. Instead, you might want to create some entirely new traditions. (See a list of possibilities in the next section of this chapter.)

Be a Parent, Not a Pushover

- Most new step-families underestimate the complexity of this daily double life. The kids have events and obligations with both families, so scheduling becomes crucial; otherwise, missteps and bad feelings will result. A good idea might be to appoint one of the adults or a responsible teen as a master scheduler (perhaps this duty could rotate), arm him or her with big calendar pages and color-coded pens for each member's events. Conflicts could be discussed and resolved at the family meetings.
- Don't treat the teens like prisoners of war whose allegiance is constantly being tested. That means no bad-mouthing, no discussing conflicts with exes in front of the kids, no complaining about how stingy or insensitive the former spouse is being.
- Especially at the beginning, discipline should probably come from the biological parent. That means it's imperative that the parent and stepparent confer and decide on the rules together—but the biological person announces and enforces those rules. The ritual of a family meeting would seem a perfect forum for talking about those rules and the consequences for breaking them. Later, after relationships have had a chance to blossom, the stepparent may become more visibly involved in setting boundaries and the penalties.

The eventual goal, of course, is family integration: Developing a sense of unity while ever mindful that this is not, and will never be, a biological family.

Step 5: Teaching

What rituals should you create?

Reflect on the role of rituals in your family. What are they? What message do they send? Do your teens appreciate them?

If meaningful rituals are lacking, begin to create them. Tradition and rituals don't just have to be for the holidays or the first of year. Take a look at the things you do every day.

Is there a way to underscore some little noticed and perhaps unspoken rituals? For instance, if you used to routinely gather for Sunday dinners but now the kids just make it when they can, perhaps there's some logic in reviving that tradition. Sure, there may be some groaning at first, but family mealtimes promote parent-teen communication. I suspect your family will come to embrace the warmth and certainty of that ritual.

Here are some random ideas on other ways you might foster healthy rituals. Use these suggestions merely as a starting point. Choose the ones that work for you. And, remember, there ought to be some fun involved, not just duty.

Create Christmas or birthday "Love Lists"

Instead of buying one another presents (or instead of buying *too many* presents), each family member makes a list of 25 reasons why the recipient is loved or valued. (Among the reasons one father received on his Love List: *You come up with weird ideas like this one.*)

Twenty-five is a lot of reasons, so the writers are sure to come up with some off-the-wall expressions as well as deep, genuine ones.

Be a Parent, Not a Pushover

Pray, meditate, or have "quiet time" together

Few group activities weave togetherness as much as just slowing down and relaxing together. Maybe you'll want to turn the lights low and light candles and perhaps incense.

Make a time to talk about heroes

Heroes tell a lot. While ours is often described as a post-heroic age, if we work at it we can still find lots of people whom we admire. Ask your teen who his or her favorites are and why. And tell about yours. Perhaps set a fixed date for doing this, maybe the first of every month, or on all major holidays named after a hero, such as Washington, Lincoln, Martin Luther King Jr., and Columbus.

Slip love notes in favorite places

None of us tell our loved ones often enough how much they mean to us. Maybe you could create a tradition of putting affectionate sticky notes—*I love you* or *You're really terrific!*—in lunch pails, under plates, inside baseball gloves or on the car dashboard or somewhere where they'll be seen in private.

Sing a perky song whenever someone wakes up grumpy

That's a fun way of sending a message about amiability.

Take control of your TV

TV is a great destroyer of traditions. It's so easy to turn it on and even eat your meals in front of it, letting everything else—conversations, art, chores, reading, listening to others—fall by the wayside.

So maybe you can assign each family member a day in which he or she is in charge of the TV. That should put an end to squabbling over what you're going to watch. It also gives you a chance to show what programs you prefer without forcing everybody else to watch your shows everyday.

Or maybe you ought to institute, say, a "No TV on Tuesdays" rule. Or some other night of the week on which the tube stays silent and talking is encouraged.

Choose a parent "date" night

The teen picks one night a month to have the undivided attention or an activity with the parents. Stake out that date and don't accept any other appointments. Do whatever the teen wants to do at home or out.

Adopt a service project

Require all family members to get involved in at least one community project per year and keep the family apprised on their progress. Maybe they can regularly do chores for an elderly person. Or work for free at the library or church. Again, you'd do well to set the example.

Designate a "Donation Day"

This is a day—say, once a week—in which all family members agree to toss their loose change or small bills into a jar. When the jar fills, discuss which charity you'd like to donate to and why.

Be a Parent, Not a Pushover

Re-learn the lesson that food doesn't really come from the grocery store

For example, set up an annual do-it-yourself berry-picking foray . . . or pumpkin harvesting . . . or even Christmas-tree cutting. Something that gets you all out of the house and involved in nature.

Show your kids the value of regularly saving and investing

Set aside some money and work with them on investing it in, say, a mutual fund or some individual stocks. You could meet at the end of each quarter to discuss the results. A number of Web sites can be helpful. See especially www.jumpStart.org for ideas on financial education for young people.

Develop your family's history

One of the greatest benefits of rituals is appreciating the importance of history and relationships in our lives. So research and talk about where your ancestors came from. Create a scrapbook and a family tree and keep it current with births, deaths, and marriages. Record stories you hear at family gatherings. You might even want to start creating an oral history by interviewing and taping the memories of your older family members. Again, there are lots of genealogical resources on the Internet that can make this as sophisticated as you wish.

Explore ethnicity

Choose one day a month to sample other cultures and cuisines. You might try Thai food one time, Mexican the next, and so on, and perhaps listen to that nation's music as you dine.

Start an "Appreciation Day"

Pick out one family member to celebrate and get everyone to commit to being particularly nice to that person on that day. Cook his favorite food, rent the movie she wants to see, play his favorite CDs, acknowledge her latest achievement. Do so not because he or she is a year older, but to show gratitude for the person he or she is.

Lessons Learned

Rituals are important not so much for what is said or done, but for the cohesiveness they build, the sense of unity that grows out of a shared, repeated experience. By creating meaningful rituals, we parents can strengthen families and help provide teens with pillars of support.

Sometimes rituals have a somber, even a spiritual overtone, but not always. Many can just as easily provide a chance to laugh together and enjoy one another's company.

Remember, perfection isn't the point. If some of your celebrations don't turn out quite as you expected, let it go. Forget the flops; those may even become memorable moments in themselves.

But when you find a celebration that works, stick with it. If it's centered on a specific day, and you're not able to do it one time, don't let it slip away. Squeeze it in as soon as you can. Such consistency will help build feelings of stability, safety, and togetherness for your teen.

Be a Parent, Not a Pushover

And with a little luck, years later that teen may look back fondly on those happy times with the family and maybe even recreate the experience with his or her children.

chapter 8

Accomplishing Goals and Solving Problems Together

*D*uncan, 16, is upset and shows it. Eyes downcast, shoulders slumped, he walks around in what seems like a perpetual funk, his expression as forlorn as his holey jeans and his Emimem t-shirt. He picks at his food, then retreats to his room and acts as if he's angry at the world—or maybe just at you.

You finally sit down with him and ask what's up. He's so glum you half-expect him to say he thinks he has a fatal disease or he's gotten official word of the imminent end of civilization.

Instead, he tells you that his buddies all seem to have their summers nailed down and their futures assured, but he doesn't. Particularly troubling is that his best buddy is going to be an Outward Bound instructor in Baja California, earning some money so he then can take a trip to Europe before school starts again in the fall. The buddy's parents, who are relatively affluent and permissive, are encouraging him, offering to match whatever he makes in his summer job.

Be a Parent, Not a Pushover

"What am I going to do all summer?" Duncan asks bitterly. "Sit around the house and watch the grass grow? I don't have the options and the freedom that he does. All I've got is nothing to do and a lot of time to do it in."

Even though it's only March, Duncan acts as if his lack of plans for the summer and his financial inability to join his friend abroad is (a) a disgrace, (b) totally hopeless, and (c) somehow your fault and (d) a certain sign that he'll never, ever do one successful thing in his entire life. He's sure to become, he thinks, a perpetually impoverished person living on the outskirts of society, or even worse, living forever with overly strict parents of decidedly modest means. In short, life is awful.

You want to practically shout: *Oh, com'on, Dunc, get a hold of yourself! You're making a big deal out of this because you're so immature. The situation is not nearly that hopeless. While we're not rich, we're not destitute, either. And though you don't always get your way, we're pretty reasonable parents. So don't be such . . . such . . . well, such a kid!*

But he *is* a kid. And you're the adult, so instead of just arguing with him, you need to give him the perspective and sense of stability that comes with age and experience. You need to teach him how to solve problems, how to work toward goals. That's one of the best things a parent can do for a child. And as a side benefit, if you help him solve his problem, you may help improve your relationship.

Teach them to fish

Teaching kids to problem-solve is akin to that old saw about giving a man a fish and thus feeding him for a day, or teaching him how to fish and thus allowing him to feed himself forever. Solve Duncan's problem for him (by just giving him the money and the okay to go to Europe) and you'll have removed the immediate source of his distress. But you won't have touched the bigger problem of getting Duncan to think for himself, set goals, and work to reach those goals.

In this chapter I want to give you a basic outline for how to work with your teens to help solve their problems . . . but more important, to get them started on the road to solving their own problems.

As I've said several times earlier, you can't really be your teen's pal. But you can be fellow problem solvers. Heaven knows, on their own teens make a lot of bad decisions. More than 87% of teen pregnancies, for example, are unintended. And teens have the highest proportion of any age group of fatal car accidents in which seats belts weren't being used.

Many teen decisions—and no few adult choices, for that matter—are based on inadequate knowledge and/or made without a great deal of thought. Teen decision-making often comes about for the wrong reasons, such as wanting to be liked or responding to a dare or just plain rebelling.

But parents can help their teens learn—and practice—setting good goals and making good decisions. And much as we talked about in Chapter 5, such decisions can bolster a teen's self-esteem.

What makes a goal?

A key element of all decision-making is: What am I seeking to do? What's my goal?

Be a Parent, Not a Pushover

The way in which the teen sets a goal has a lot to do with how successful he or she is likely to be. A vague or sloppily worded goal may be worse than none at all. That's because the teen will feel badly at not accomplishing the goal, even though failure may have been inherent in the way it was structured.

Here are ways to make goals effective:

Write them down

Verbal goals, as Yogi Berra might have said, are only as good as the paper they're written on. Getting your teen to put them on paper will give the goals more force and help avoid confusion later on. Writing down goals makes us be more specific about them. We also can refer to them during the year and see how we measured up.

Express them positively

"Drive without a traffic ticket for one year" is much better than "Don't make stupid driving mistakes."

Make them measurable

Be as specific as possible in describing what the teen wants to accomplish. So instead vowing to "Be a better person," she should state more precisely what she will do, such as "Refrain from gossiping for 30 days" or "Get up by 7 a.m. Monday through Friday in order to get more tasks accomplished." If the teen wants to "do well" in biology class, it will be hard to say at semester's end if that goal was achieved. But if the objective is to raise the grade from a "C+" to a "B," you and the teen will know for certain if that was done.

For true measurability, teens also need to designate a time-frame. So they should specify target completion dates. If they achieve all conditions of a measurable goal, then they can take comfort in its achievement. If they fail, they can adjust it or analyze the reason for failure and then plan corrective action.

Keep them realistic

Set goals the teen is capable of reaching, even though it will be a challenge. Keep the immediate goals small and achievable. If the goal is too large, the task can be overwhelming, and it won't seem as if the youngster is making as much progress as it would if you broke those down into increments.

Setting goals at the right level is a skill that comes with practice. If a teen sets a goal too high (or lets others influence him to set them too high), he or she will be doomed to frustration. Striving to score 100% of every test at school, for example, is admirable but not very do-able. Setting them too low may suggest the teen fears failure. So try to set them so they are slightly out of the student's immediate grasp but not so high that they're unachievable.

For instance, if your teen sadly complains, "I'm shy. I want to be popular, but I just know that I'll be rejected. I don't know how to speak up for myself. I'll never have any friends." The situation may not be as grim as the teen suggests, but it's still a long-term problem, not susceptible to the quick fix. So the goal might be "To win one new friend this year" instead of "Become 'popular' this semester." Then figure out a way to increase the chances of meeting that potential friend.

Be a Parent, Not a Pushover

Set priorities

As the Chinese philosopher Lao Tzu said, "A journey of a thousand miles begins with one step." So when your teen has several goals, help him or her give each a priority. This directs efforts toward the most important ones. Similarly, breaking big goals into bite-sized chunks is usually a good idea. If the teen's goal is to get at least a "B" in chemistry, encourage him or her to work on scoring well on the first assignment, then the second, then the first test, then the mid-term, and so on.

Focus on performance, not outcomes

Goals based on outcomes ("Become class president as well as president of the student council" or "Score 20 or more points in each varsity basketball game") are vulnerable to failure because of factors the kid can't control—for instance, perhaps the school principal has a role in selecting presidents of the class and the student council, and he doesn't want one student holding both honors. Or, this year's new basketball schedule is so tough nobody on his or her team is likely to score that many points.

Better would be to set goals over which the teen will have as much control as possible. For example, "Get active in student government by running for office" or "Improve my points-per-game average by at least 5 points."

Getting teens involved

Young people often have a lot of good ideas about how to deal with problems. When they can contribute to decisions, they also are likely to follow through with improved behavior.

Parents who persist in solving their teen's problems or doing their decision-making for them only make it more difficult for their child to become a responsible adult.

Unwanted parental control has two outcomes, both bad. One, the kids may never learn to stand on their own two feet. As adults, they may be unable to make decisions and may not even be able to live away from home. Or, two, they may rebel and perhaps misbehave in ways the parents had tried to prevent, such as abusing alcohol or drugs. On the other hand, parents who gradually let the child take responsibility are helping prepare the kid for adulthood.

The kind of parenting that gets teens to do what you want in the short term—such as nagging, harsh punishment, or insistence on the parents getting their own way—doesn't usually do much to teach responsibility and maturity. But parents who take a longer view are more likely to involve the children in setting rules and solving problems.

Candidates for problem solving

Any situation that can cause trouble for parent or teen—whether it's household chores, homework, peers, or sibling antagonism—can be a candidate for joint problem solving. In such cases, parents should involve their teen in brainstorming solutions. That's a good way to lead them to making good decisions.

Bullying, for example, is a common high school problem, with 15% of students said to be regularly either the intimidator or the victim. Though adults often see it as a harmless rite of passage, for many students the teasing, taunting, rumormongering, threatening, hitting, and stealing creates a climate of torment that robs the school years of much of their joy. Parents often are unaware of the problem, and students tend to feel that adult intervention is rare and ineffective.

But need it be? First, you need to know about the problem. Find out if there's ongoing physical or verbal mistreatment. So this involves getting your kid to level with you. If you find out he or she is bullying or being bullied, then you can work with him or her to try to put an end to it. While much of bullying has its root in early childhood and general self-esteem, you can come up with a plan. Defensive tactics—from assertiveness training to avoidance—exist. Work with your teen, as well as with teachers and school officials, to see if this can be reduced or eliminated.

Amazing results can occur if you have a worthwhile goal, if you know what's required to accomplish it, and if everyone participates. For instance, a new Southern California program I'm involved with and excited about is called Compact for Success.

Seventh-graders in the relatively poor, overwhelmingly minority Sweetwater Union High School District and their parents can sign up for the Compact. If the students meet specific performance expectations—starting in grade seven and continuing through high school—they earn this guarantee: admission to San Diego State University with a full-tuition scholarship. Students must commit to maintaining a 3.0 GPA, taking college-prep classes, passing math and English placement tests, and taking the SAT or ACT test, among other requirements. And parents must agree to monitor and support their kids' progress and attend meetings and go on college visits. For their part, educators agree to provide funding, tutoring, and intervention programs.

The aim, of course, is to get kids and their parents focusing early on college, before the kids even reach high school. The program just began in the year 2000, so we won't know the initial outcome for another few years, but early indications are that students and their parents are enthusiastically on board, with more than half the eligible seventh-graders signing up so far for this program that's believed to be unique in the nation.

Steps to a decision

Let's look in more detail at the steps to decision-making:

1. Describe the problem in detail. Let's say the problem is that your daughter hasn't been washing the car weekly, which is a major part of her household chores. You could make a decree ("*You* will *wash the car!*") or prescribe some arbitrary punishment ("*There will be no renting of movie videos unless that car is clean*").

But a better idea would be to ask her why this is such a problem.

She may say, *With soccer and homework and helping with preparations for the school dance, I just haven't had any time to relax. Also, I just* hate *getting all wet and getting my hair messed up. Washing the car is just an awful job.*

2. Tell how you both feel about the problem. Listening to each other's views is important but often isn't easy. We each

get so entrenched in our viewpoint that it's hard to acknowledge what the other feels. Yet when people feel heard, they're more likely to work toward a solution. So you might say, *I get really frustrated when the car isn't washed. It's part of your duties to the household, and because I use the car on business, it reflects poorly on me when I show up in a filthy car.* The teen might reply, *But it takes such a long time and makes me feel so awful. I'd rather do anything but that.*

3. Brainstorm possible solutions. List as many ways as possible to deal with the problem. Don't critique the alternatives yet, just toss them out there, trying to generate as many ideas as possible. For instance, in this case the alternatives might include:

- Leaving the car dirty
- Switching the family chores around so someone else washes the car and your daughter gets a different household assignment
- Taking turns washing the car
- Finding the money to get the car professionally washed
- Washing the car at a coin-operated, self-serve car wash that may involve less time and hassle than washing it at home

Brainstorming is an area where a parent, with vastly more experience than the teen, can often make the greatest contribution. Parents often are better at foreseeing the potential outcomes and consequences. What will happen if you leave the car dirty? If you decide to pay to have the car washed, for example, where will that money come from and what will be shortchanged? If you change the assignment of household chores, will the newly designated car washer have the time and ability to handle the job? Is someone else in the family willing to take on the car-washing task?

4. Try one of the alternatives. Test one to try for a specific period of time. And be as clear as possible about the nature of the test. For example, if the plan were to get the car professionally washed, you must jointly decide how you would raise the money? Who would take it to the carwash? What chores would the teen do in lieu of washing the car? It may be a good idea to write down the agreement, not as a threat but as a record. To lessen the risk of confusion and to affirm responsibility, get each participant to repeat what he or she has agreed to do.

You might also want to invent a way to nudge each other if someone should fail to follow through. Lapses are likely. And a major complaint of teens is that their parents nag them. So a good idea when adopting a plan is to say something like, *Great idea. But how will we remind each other if we get busy and forget?*

Getting the teen involved in the reminding process takes the sting out of "nagging." Maybe he or she will just want you to say something. Or perhaps put a note on the refrigerator or on a family-room bulletin board. If reminders don't help, then the solution isn't working and another must be tried.

5. Evaluate the results. Name a time—say, one month later—in which you will check back to see how the plan is

working. If it isn't, then you together will select another idea from the list to try.

Important: Parents must show respect for themselves and for the process by following through and not letting the kid slough off. Whatever you do, don't just let lapses slide. Let your child know that you expect him to keep the agreement. That doesn't mean criticizing and calling the teen names. It does mean pointing out the sanctity of the agreement and requiring all to adhere to it or participate in coming up with a new one.

In short, involving teens in solving problems and in follow-through teaches cooperation and good decision making. It allows parents to hold onto their power while the teens also retain theirs. It gets the current job done but also helps prepare the kids to become responsible adults.

Duncan revisited

In the case of our friend Duncan, the unhappy teen who sees himself without a European trip and a future, how should you proceed?

You'll recall that he wants to go to Europe with his friend. But he doesn't have the money or a handle on a summer job that will give him the money. Nor does he have any assurance that you'd let him go even if he—or you—could afford it. What to do?

Well, instead of allowing Duncan to just wallow in self-pity, get him started on thinking through the dilemma.

First, you will need to sit down with him and . . .

1. Describe the problem in detail. From Duncan's standpoint, the problem is that he fears wasting the summer and missing a chance to go to Europe with his friend.

You might try to help him break that goal down into its parts. Is it possible, for example, to have a fruitful summer but not earn money and not go to Europe? Would it suffice if he could get a job and earn some money toward his education, and think about Europe later? How much of this problem is social (keeping up with his globe-trotting friend) and how much is about avoiding boredom (by having something worthwhile to do over the summer)?

Plus, quite apart from his druthers, there's some information you and he don't have yet, such as how much would it cost to go to Europe? How much could he expect to earn? How late in the summer could a decision still be made to go to Europe? And, of course, are you even going to agree to allow him to join another teenager for an unsupervised European odyssey? Where in Europe would they be going? How long would they stay?

Sorting through all this you come up with this description of the problem: Duncan needs something to do this summer, and, it's hoped, something that will earn him money. He'd like to use that money to go to Europe, but you're not convinced the Europe trip would be a good idea, financially or otherwise.

2. Tell how you both feel about the problem. Duncan says it's extremely important for him to get a summer job, but upon questioning, admits it's less critical that he accompany his friend, though, of course, that would be terrific.

Be a Parent, Not a Pushover

Steps/solutions for attaining Goal No. 1 (getting a job):

Duncan will:
__ inquire what other kids are doing
__check the classified ads
__ask school counselors
__apply at an on-line job bank
__ask at the hardware store where his brother used to work
__consider starting own summer business of cutting lawns, doing odd jobs, etc.

You will:
__inquire of your friends about businesses that are or may be hiring
__ask your employer about any summer openings

Steps/solutions for attaining Goal No. 2 (going to Europe):

—Parent will pay (ruled out).
—Duncan will raise sufficient money (must follow completion of Goal No. 1 ... and subject to parental veto if adult supervision issue is not satisfactorily addressed)
—Duncan will obtain further information, including (1) deadline for buying tickets at cheapest fare (2) how much the friend/friend's parents believe the journey will cost (3) a tentative itinerary for the hoped-for trip
—You will review family finances with an eye toward what, if anything, you could contribute to the trip

❧

His friend's parents are willing to pay for their son; Duncan doesn't understand why you're such a cheapskate.

You say: *Money is tight around the household right now, but even if it weren't, I think (a) giving a teen a large sum for such travel is not character-building and is against my principles and (b) 16 years old is too young to travel to Europe without an adult present.*

So not only are you not inclined to give him the money, you're also not likely to match whatever he might raise. You say you think waiting until he can afford to pay for most of it himself would make the journey more meaningful and that he'd then be more mature and would get more out of the trip. You make it clear you're not likely to pay for him to go now.

3. Brainstorm possible solutions. So, there are two issues: Getting a job and (maybe) going to Europe. You need to help him think through each and define limiting factors, such as time and money.

4. *Evaluate the results.* You and Duncan agree to report back in two weeks on the results in both cases. On Goal No. 1, depending on what the two of you find out, Duncan can decide which job possibilities to pursue.

Regarding Goal No. 2, you're clear about your skepticism, but you're willing to keep an open mind until more information is in hand.

If Duncan finds out the cutoff date for ordering the Europe tickets, that will give you a deadline by which to ultimately decide about the trip. He's also going to find out the approximate cost and you're going to review your own finances.

But, of course, you reiterate that you're not favorably inclined unless Duncan can raise all the money himself *and* someone other than just his 16-year-old friend is going along. You strongly suggest that in all likelihood this trip should be postponed until Duncan is older, has more money, and has a better plan.

So what's the upshot? Well, Duncan may still be peeved at you for not coming up with the money for the trip or with some sort of guaranteed job. But at least he knows where you stand and what he has to do. There's less reason for him to go around mad at you and the world.

He knows he has to get a job for the summer and has some ideas of where to start. And if he is to go to Europe, he knows he has to earn most or all of the money, and he has to have a better plan than just heading off with another teenage boy without any specifics.

He may not be a totally happy camper, but he at least understands the rules of the campground.

What to do?

Apart from applying the decision-making template, what else can you do to help your kid set and achieve goals? There's a lot you can do. Here are some suggestions:

Get them in the decision-making habit

Give your teens lots of opportunities, starting with fairly simple ones. Let's say you cede to them the issue of whether the family should get a new pet. You have some definite ideas about that, but you're willing to negotiate. So you ask the teen to think over the issue and answer the questions:

- Why do we need a new cat, dog, bird, or whatever?
- Are there alternatives we haven't thought of? Maybe become a foster parent for a dog or cat from the humane society to see how we liked the animal? Or get a "loaner" from a pet store or breeder?
- Which kind of animal would work best and why?
- Where would we get such a creature?
- What are the consequences of adopting this pet, such as cost, cleanup, division of responsibilities?
- When could or should we do this?

Show your teen how to question the need, weigh the options, and consider alternatives and potential outcomes. Be supportive, friendly, and ready to bail him or her out if necessary. But otherwise, let him make the call.

Avoid a "You can have any opinion as long as it agrees with mine" stance

Understand that making decisions is more of an art than a science, and thus someone else's decision will be based in part on that person's tastes and needs. So it may not match the choice you would have made. But that's O.K. so long as it's not a terribly wrong choice. In other words, it's more important that you support the kid's ability to make a decision than have your own preferences ratified.

Set up some ground rules

You can't let the child do something that's clearly harmful or unacceptable. Explain that to him or her. That way, you'll reassert your authority but also provide a bit of a safety net.

Emphasize that decisions = consequences

To a teen, smoking cigarettes may make them feel grownup and cool—but do they really understand the many downsides of that habit? Or of not wearing seatbelts? Or of indiscriminate sexual activity?

How do you make such connections clear in the busy, confused teenage mind? Two ways: first, by talking about smoking, seat belts, and, yes, even sex. Second, by making clear the correlation between actions and consequences in other areas. This is what is known as accountability.

Take punishment, for instance. If the teen comes home at 11:45 p.m. when he or she was supposed to be home by 10, don't just drop it. Follow through with the punishment, whatever it is. You'll be sending the message that there are boundaries, we do need to follow them, and bad outcomes occur when we don't. The punishment doesn't need to be harsh, but it needs to be prompt and clearly stated.

Or, take reward. Discuss your teen's long- and short-term goals about money: What does she want to buy and save for? A computer? Clothes? College?

Show them how to save. Talk about the wise use of credit, about what goes into buying and maintaining a car, paying for college, living on their own. Again, you're showing them something topical and practical about money management, but on a deeper level, you're also teaching them how life works: There is no free lunch, and every action or inaction has its consequences.

Stress consideration of others

Underscore also how the decisions they make should take into account the effects on others. Let's say the decision involves something simple, like choosing the site for a family picnic. The kid is likely to choose a place he or she likes, perhaps a favorite park or a site that's near an amusement park. Remind him that their grandparents are involved, too, and there may not be enough shade for the old folks. Or it's not geographically appropriate for some other family member. List the other possibilities and try to guide him toward the one that has the most advantages—and the fewest disadvantages— for the most people.

Show them that not deciding is not always an option

If a student can't decide which college to apply to, he or she may miss the deadline. Sometimes all the good solutions disappear if we don't act promptly. Help your teen resign himself to the fact that perfection is rarely attainable and is rarely a reason for infinite delay.

Be a Parent, Not a Pushover

Listen with an open mind

When your teen talks to you about his or her problems and concerns, be a respectful audience. Don't dismiss youthful worries as trivial.

Help keep them on track

Often teens have a general sense of where they want to go but they lose sight of the steps—not all of them are fun and entertaining—that will take them there. That's where your more mature mind can help.

Say, for instance, the problem is that his American history teacher is "so-o-o-o boring" and that social science is "so-o-o-o dull" that your teen is inattentive, perhaps cutting class, or even failing these subjects. After all, he says, he wants to be an engineer, and engineers don't need to know anything about history and the social sciences. Well, no, maybe they don't, but they do need to get to college, and getting poor marks in high school history and social science isn't the way to do that.

So you need to be firm in reminding the kid of the ultimate goal. Help him clarify his sense of purpose, help him to see the role that difficult subjects and difficult situations play in reaching personal goals.

In fact, performance in school is a common conflict between parents and teens. Lecturing your teen or using punishment to motivate him to get better grades probably isn't going to help. Strong-arm tactics likely will be interpreted as intrusive and over-controlling.

Instead, while making it clear that you want what is best for him, talk about his goals—and not just the short-term goal of passing the course. Don't focus just on the grades themselves. Instead, concentrate on what the reward is for good grades. His performance in school is a means to an end. So what does he want out of life? How does getting a decent grade in history and social science relate to that goal?

Be a model problem-solver

As I've said many times elsewhere in this book, children are very careful observers of our behavior, then they mirror our actions. What kind of example are you showing in how you make decisions?

Do you make arbitrary decisions without much thought? Do you back away from challenges because of fear? Do you cut off debate and assert your authority to make family decisions because "I'm the boss"?

Lessons Learned

Teaching your kids to solve problems fosters a sense of ownership of and control over their own lives. They're then less likely to be overwhelmed by everyday problems because they have the inner resources.

It's a bit of an act of faith—especially in a household where rancor, not rationality, is king—to believe that sitting down and sharing feelings with a young person will yield solutions to common problems. But trust me on this: Give it a shot, and you're likely to be surprised at the results.

Be a Parent, Not a Pushover

And finding you can reach an understanding about little things—who should take out the trash, say, or how to set the Saturday night curfew—may revolutionize your whole approach to teen-rearing. If you find you can actually listen to one another, think of the *possibilities!* You no longer have to engage in a power struggle, no longer need to determine who's the victor and who's the vanquished, no longer just mete out punishment because to give praise would somehow encourage disrespect. You can instead put your energy into searching for the sort of solutions that will serve you both.

There's always the chance that in helping your teenagers solve their problems you'll help yourself as well.

chapter 9

Shedding Stress and Finding Peace

*C*hange, or even worry about change, is what causes stress. Now I ask you: *Who* changes more than teens? Their bodies, their brains, their self-image, their place in the family, in the work force, in society are all quickly changing. So—*surprise!*—teens are probably the most stressed-out of us all.

Not that adults don't have pressure. But teens are practically swimming in it—and often we parents make it worse. Besides, teens often can't cope very well because, emotionally, they're really still kids.

Stress appears to affects boys and girls differently. But both may go into stress overload, which can lead to anxiety, withdrawal, aggression, physical illness, and drug or alcohol abuse. But the good news is that loving, firm involvement by you can help protect your youngster from serious problems.

In this chapter I'm going to explain the causes of stress, how it shows up, and most important, how you can help your kid better manage it.

Be a Parent, Not a Pushover

We experience stress when we perceive a changing situation as dangerous, difficult, or painful. That pretty much describes the entire teen years. Almost everything is dangerous, difficult, or painful—school, friendships, parents, dating, money, activities, the future, to name just a few.

Sometimes this results from pressure from the outside (needing to score high on the SATs in order to get into the "right" college) or sometimes from within (wanting so badly to be liked and admired despite being socially clumsy and having pimples, to boot.) So it's easy to feel overwhelmed.

A bit of stress, of course, can be good. Without it, we probably wouldn't push ourselves to do our best. We all know the stress of a deadline, for instance. But we also know that without deadlines, we'd probably not get much done.

You can't totally protect your child from stress. Even if you could, that wouldn't be wise; they're going to face plenty of stress as adults and you want them to be prepared. You also want them to be motivated, too, and try to excel.

That's why health professionals talk about stress management, not stress elimination. But chronic stress can affect children physically, emotionally, and psychologically. That's what you want to reduce or eliminate.

It's a jungle out there

Kids have plenty to cope with. Teen angst is almost certainly more severe than when we were kids. Major sources of stress include academic demands, parents' financial problems, changes in schools and neighborhoods, peer pressure, death of a loved one, separation or divorce of parents, and sometimes even violence in the schools and communities.

Add to that mix the pressure and confusion our culture puts on kids in the form of ongoing exposure to violence on TV, in the movies, and in some rap music and hard rock lyrics; terrorism, the threat of AIDS, the danger of nuclear holocaust, the depiction of sex at an early age, and of course, the scourge of drugs.

Then there's economic tension. Facing intensified competition for schools and jobs, many teens worry, for instance, that they won't be able to make a good living. Some have been raised amid such affluence that they secretly fear they'll never match the achievements of their parents, an aspiration among American youth for generations.

Are you contributing?

What's more, a lot of us unwittingly turn our home life into yet another source of stress. Dr. David Ryan Marks, author of *Raising Stable Kids in an Unstable World* calls this the "mouse mill," a pint-sized version of the rat race that most adults know all too well. We don't do this to our kids intentionally. It's just that we want "more" for them: more than we had, perhaps, or more money, more power, more recognition. As a result, we encourage—perhaps *push*—them to pack their schedules with academics, sports, ballet, music, karate, school and civic groups, you name it, anything that might help them stand out from their peers and secure a good future.

Too often, maybe compensating for our own shortcomings, we place unrealistic expectations on our kids and foster a hectic lifestyle in which staying home and being average is not an option. Major stress results. And sooner or later, the energy drain on the teen's system will cause the body to fall behind in its repair work. Thus, the body will lose its fight to stay healthy in the face of the increased energy the teen is expending.

The Youth Stress Scale

In the following table you can look up changes in your teen's life and calculate how much stress value each is contributing. Note any item that has been experienced in the past 12 months. Then total the score:

Stress Scale for Youth*

Stress Event Value

1. Death of spouse, parent, boyfriend/girlfriend........ 100
2. Divorce (of self or parents)......................... 65
3. Puberty... 65
4. Pregnancy (or causing pregnancy)................... 65
5. Marital separation or breakup with boyfriend/girlfriend.. 60
6. Jail term or probation.............................. 60
7. Death of family member (apart from spouse, parent, or boyfriend/girlfriend)......................... 60
8. Broken engagement................................. 55
9. Engagement.. 50
10. Serious personal injury or illness.....................45
11. Marriage...45

---

* Adapted from the "Social Readjustment Rating Scale" by Thomas Holmes and Richard Rahe, in the *Journal of Psychosomatic Research*, Copyright 1967, vol. II, p. 214. Used by permission of Pergamon Press Ltd.

12. Entering college or beginning next level of school
(starting junior high or high school) 45
13. Change in independence or responsibility.....................45
14. Any drug or alcohol use..45
15. Fired at work or expelled from school..........................45
16. Change in alcohol or drug use 45
17. Reconciliation with mate, family or
boyfriend/girlfriend...40
18. Trouble at school..40
19. Serious health problem of a family member 40
20. Working while attending school...................................35
21. Working more than 40 hours per week.........................35
22. Changing course of study...35
23. Change in frequency of dating.....................................35
24. Sexual adjustment problems (confusion
of sexual identity)...35
25. Gain of new family member (new baby born
or parent remarries)..35
26. Change in work responsibilities...................................35
27. Change in financial state 30
28. Death of close friend (not family member) 30
29. Change to a different kind of work...............................30
30. Change in number of arguments with mate,
family or friends...30
31. Sleep less than 8 hours per night 25
32. Trouble with in-laws or boyfriend's/girlfriend's family 25
33. Oustanding personal achievement (awards,
grades, etc.) 25
34. Mate or parents start or stop working...........................20
35. Begin or end school..20
36. Change in living conditions (visitors in the home,
remodeling house, change in roommates)...................20

37. Change in personal habits (start or stop a habit, such as smoking or dieting) 20
38. Chronic allergies 20
39. Trouble with the boss 20
40. Change in work hours 15
41. Change in residence 15
42. Change to a new school (other than graduation) 10
43. Presently in pre-menstrual period 15
44. Change in religious activity 15
45. Going into debt (you or your family) 10
46. Change in frequency of family gatherings 10
47. Vacation 10
48. Presently in winter holiday season 10
49. Minor violation of the law 5

Total score = _____

Scoring: If your teen has experienced total stress within the last 12 months of 250 or greater, he or she may be overstressed. Persons with low stress tolerance may be overstressed at levels as low as 150.

Physical symptoms of emotional issues

Kids show stress in different ways. Its impact depends on a child's personality, maturity, and style of coping. It's not always obvious when kids are feeling overtaxed or what the cause is. Sometimes a little detective work is required.

Take Emma. Her mom is caring and wise. But she was also going through a divorce, which is enough to test anyone's wisdom and care-giving nature. She brought 13-year-old Emma to see me. Emma had always been a good student and a good kid, but lately had been angry, uncharacteristically saying to her mom hurtful things like "Leave me alone. I hate you."

Emma denied she felt anxiety about the divorce. "I'm fine," she said, adding that she's sorry for her outbursts and acknowledging a need to control her temper. But the truth was that she was not fine. In fact, she had been experiencing severe stomach pain and nausea for more than six months.

Part of the treatment, of course, was to get her a complete physical. As I imagined, the tests came back negative: There was no organic reason for her pain. But both her mom and I knew she wasn't pretending to be sick.

After talking to them both, I began to see some possible explanations for the symptoms. The Father-Daughter Picnic was coming up, and Emma had invited her uncle, not her dad, to be her escort. Her father no longer lives at home and travels a lot on business. Emma made it sound as if he would have been too busy to attend and that she understood, but clearly she was angry with her dad. When pressed, she admitted that she didn't want his feelings to be hurt, but she wasn't willing to have him let her down one more time by canceling at the last minute.

Soon after the picnic, Emma was celebrating her birthday. And that also conflicted her. Not wanting to disappoint her dad but protecting herself from disappointment was creating a great deal of inner conflict.

Be a Parent, Not a Pushover

Once we figured out what the problem was, her mother and I focused on improving Emma's coping and problem-solving skills, which got better. Not surprisingly, the stomach pains and nausea also subsided.

The point is, dealing with stress can be difficult, but with love, patience, and understanding, it's do-able. We can help our kids become physically and psychologically healthy adults.

Stress differs by gender

It was somewhat unusual that Emma's stress took the form of extreme physical discomfort. But the fact that family relationships were the cause of the girl's suffering is not uncommon. Males and females show distinctly different patterns of stress. Adolescent girls are more likely to have stress over their relations with parents and friends, while the sources of stress in boys are more commonly school performance or other factors outside of their social relationships, such as a move to another home. That's because, research suggests, girls are more invested than boys in relationships as a source of emotional support and personal identity.

A study at Iowa State University and the University of North Carolina found major gender differences. While boys reported slightly more depressed feelings than girls prior to age 13, that trend reversed itself with age. Symptoms of depression rose for girls until at least age 17 and in many cases into young adulthood. Overall, symptoms of depression remained lower in boys than in girls and were relatively stable.

The study concluded that teenage girls are more at risk for depression for at least two main reasons: One, they undergo more life changes than boys and for yet unknown reasons, they are more vulnerable to negative life events.

The research also showed that the role of the mother was highly important for girls, but not for boys. Girls with supportive mothers reported fewer depressive symptoms than girls who lacked strong maternal backing. Supportive mothers showed warmth toward their daughters, listened carefully, and made a strong effort to talk and socialize with their daughters.

Is your kid over-stressed?

Symptoms vary. Here's a checklist of possible effects:

Is your teen over-stressed?

He or she may be if he *feels* . . .

    __ depressed
    __ edgy
    __ guilty
    __ tired
    __ listless
    __ achy, especially in chest, shoulders, back, and neck

If he or she . . .

    __ laughs or cries for no obvious reason
    __ sees only the negative side of many situations
    __ resents other people
    __ blames others for bad things happening to the teen
    __ fails to get out and do things
    __ acts with uncharacteristic carelessness

Be a Parent, Not a Pushover

 __ experiences a sharp drop-off in school
  performance
 __ can't concentrate

If he or she complains of . . .
 __ headaches
 __ stomachaches
 __ trouble sleeping
 __ frequent nightmares
 __ lack of interest in the outside world
 __ anxiety
 __ panic attacks when he can't catch his breath
 __ rashes

Note also that other, pre-existing chronic conditions can be worsened by stress. Particularly look for any signs of worsening of asthma, hay fever, migraines, and gastrointestinal illness like colitis, irritable bowel syndrome, and peptic ulcer.

If your child has more than a few of the symptoms mentioned above, especially if they continue for weeks or months, you need to take action. You might start by looking in the mirror.

Help your teen by helping yourself

The most important step you can take to help your teen to better handle stress is to handle it better yourself. It's best if you can stay calm even when your teen is being unreasonable.

Do you remember in Chapter 3 where I talked about how teens tend to value action over words? If you want your teen to live a sane, balanced life, set the example. "Do as I say, not do as I do" just won't hack it.

So, for starters, examine your own behavior by asking yourself:

Am I reinforcing anxiety in my teen?

You may be if you're manic while continually urging him or her to be calm and well-ordered. In studies of families who have experienced severely traumatic circumstances, such as earthquakes or war, the best predictor of how well a child copes is how well the parents cope. And as mentioned earlier, marital conflict is particularly unsettling for kids. So you and your spouse should be setting the standard for how issues are dealt with.

Am I developing and modeling stress-management skills?

Learn to manage your own stress better. Teens and parents who learn stress-management skills feel less helpless. And the further good news is that many options are available, including exercise, a healthy diet, yoga, meditation, art therapy, visualization, biofeedback, and psychological counseling.

What you can do for your teen's stress

But before consulting a professional, you might want to consider what *you* can do to set a good example and other steps you can take to help your kid.

Kids' worries and concerns increase sharply as they move from the ages of 13 to 18, psychologists believe. But as Dr. Hans Selye, the father of modern stress management, pointed out, it's not so much "the event but the perception of the event" that creates stress. Being older and wiser, you should be in a position to lessen your teen's stress by being realistic about problems and their solutions.

Some actions you can take:

Keep open the lines of communication

Teens feel better about themselves when they have a good relationship with their parents. Talk with them often, following the communication practices suggested in Chapter 3. Be available for guidance and advice.

Warn of pending crises

If you know of a possible big shock ahead—say, a health crisis, a divorce, or a move—let the teen know as early as possible in order to lessen the shock. If possible, spread out events so children can adapt gradually.

Help allay their long-term fears

Many kids worry about big, long-range questions, such as career and livelihood, romance and marriage, health and safety. Even if they don't talk about these, you *should*, perhaps indirectly. You might want to point out that although you and other adults wrestled with these big-caliber questions when young, eventually you got jobs and mates and avoided serious health setbacks. If need be, encourage them to also get advice from a school counselor, religious adviser, psychologist or doctor.

Guard against trying to live through your teen's achievements

A common parental tendency is to seek to live vicariously through a teen by insisting he or she excel in academics, sports, or other pursuits in which you missed the mark.

Be candid about your frustrations

It's important to be frank about your setbacks as well as your successes when you talk to your teen. Kids need to know that parents have failures, too. Show how you deal with those.

Help them seek balance

Support healthy involvement in sports, the arts, spiritual pursuits, friendships and community service. (And heed the same advice yourself.) Encourage your teen to exercise and eat regularly, avoid too much caffeine, learn relaxation techniques, and try to be proactive about situations that cause stress (*e.g.*, take a speech class if addressing people causes anxiety).

Encourage the doing of a competent job, not a perfect one

He or she will feel better about himself if he knows it's okay to let go of perfectionism, that it's all right to make mistakes once in a while.

Urge them to take lots of breaks from stressful situations

Support them in activities such as listening to music, hiking, spending time with pets, and writing. No matter how busy their schedule, they (and you) need time to play and to relax.

Be a Parent, Not a Pushover

Writing down thoughts in a journal or diary may also help relieve emotional stress.

Discourage them from becoming "control freaks"

Help your teen compile a list of things that cause him/her stress. Discuss the fact that some, perhaps a majority of the listed items are beyond control. But help them to say "no" to things they can't or don't want to do—for example, taking too many courses and/or working too many hours at a part-time job.

Don't push them beyond their limits

Well-intentioned efforts to help your kids, such as pushing them to apply for the very best colleges, could put too much pressure on them. Show patience by letting them select and strive toward their own goals. Show acceptance and encouragement for whatever they decide. Don't compare them or their achievements to others.

Monitor their stress

Listen carefully and watch for signs of overloading mentioned above. Constant striving to live up to high expectations—theirs or others—can be very stressful. With every new course, new teacher, new school, new team, or even new hobby, questions of achievement and performance arise. Especially for the sensitive child, each new endeavor brings with it the terrifying risk of being inadequate or mediocre.

Help them learn organization and time-management skills

Stress will probably be reduced if you can show the teen, for example, how large projects are less overwhelming if broken down into manageable steps, how to set priorities, how to say "no" gracefully, and how to take breaks from work. Another habit worth encouraging is to write things down. Having a daily list of what he or she expects to do may help the teen be more realistic about his schedule.

Encourage them to have fun with their peers

Children who lack such friendships are at risk for developing stress-related difficulties. Encourage your teen to spend time with enjoyable people without the pressures of school, work, or difficult relationships. Urge teens to seek the company of those who are optimistic and have high self-esteem.

Nurture their spirituality

Religious or spiritual beliefs give us a context larger than ourselves, and that can provide perspective when we're deeply stressed. Spirituality doesn't necessarily involve a formal place of worship. This can mean just meditating, communing with nature, or taking time out for reflection on something more than life's everyday problems.

Help them eat right

Unfortunately, we tend to turn to "comfort" foods—such as macaroni and cheese, pizza, and ice cream—when we're stressed. These high-fat foods are usually the worst possible choice because they can make us feel lethargic and less able to deal with stress, not to mention driving up blood pressure and raising serum cholesterol.

A better solution: Low-fat, high, carbohydrate-rich meals with plenty of fruits and vegetables. Thus, a better choice of comfort foods would be, for example, baked sweet potatoes, minestrone soup, or sautéed vegetables over rice.

While sugar, a carbohydrate, tends to calm us at first, it leaves the bloodstream rapidly, causing us to "crash." Better are complex carbohydrates, such as pasta, beans, and lentils, which can soothe without the resulting "fall."

Be clear—in words and behavior—about how dangerous it is to try to escape via drugs and alcohol

These may be readily available to the teen and look like an easy out, but they just add new problems, such as addiction and health concerns. But, again, you'll need to model reasonable behavior. If you're self-medicating with liquor, for example, your words will have scant effect.

Learn all you can to help him or her deal with stress

For example, go to the Web site of the American Academy of Child and Adolescent Psychiatry <www.aacap.org> and click on "Facts for Families." Or to Focus Adolescent Services <www.fousas.com> and click on "Helping Teenagers with Stress." Both sites provide a wealth of information not only on stress but many other facets of adolescent and teen life.

Aid them in finding someone to talk to if conditions worsen

If they don't seem at ease talking to you or someone else in your family, perhaps they should see a minister/priest/rabbi, school counselor, or doctor. Consult with a child or adolescent psychiatrist or other mental health professional if signs of stress continue.

Depression

It's a danger sign when stress becomes too much to deal with and your teen just feels like giving up. At worst, he or she could be sliding toward clinical depression, and that's serious. Often frighteningly persistent, it can be disabling, even life-threatening.

Again, there appear to be gender differences. By age 14 to 15, girls are twice as likely to suffer from depression, a gender difference that persists into adulthood. One in four girls is said to exhibit depressive symptoms—that's a rate 50% higher than in boys.

Such youth can be at high risk for suicide. (Adolescent girls report alarmingly high rates of thinking about suicide. While boys are more likely to commit suicide, girls attempt it more often.)

Clinical depression has been linked to an inherited imbalance in brain chemicals, although family environment also is a contributing factor. Depression is in part a disorder of relationships. The depressed person withdraws and breaks connections with the larger traditions of which we are a part, such as family, culture, and religion. Part of the antidote is strengthening those relationships.

Be a Parent, Not a Pushover

For instance, Mary, usually a bright 13-year-old, was getting failing grades, not turning in her school work, and becoming sullen and withdrawn. When she was tested by the school psychologist, the teen replied "I don't know" to most of the questions or just stayed silent. When the psychologist met with Mary and her parents to discuss the results, the psychologist said, "Mary scored in the borderline range of intellectual functioning. These children make wonderful employees— they're very hardworking."

When they left the office, Mary began to cry, "Mom, she thinks I'm stupid." That's when her mother brought Mary to me to see what was at the root of her academic underachievement. Mary had always been shy, but now she didn't even want to talk to her parents or siblings. She had become more and more withdrawn until she was clearly depressed.

She confided in me that she'd been under a lot of pressure before being tested by the psychologist. School was difficult, she said, she was having problems with friends, and she was beginning to feel as if she could "never do anything right." She was driven to get good grades, to excel in her music recital, and to be "popular" with her peers, so much so that all this stress was affecting her emotional health and her ability to learn. "I'm so afraid of being wrong," she said.

This chronic stress had become such an overwhelming burden that she became "brain-locked" and began to believe that she really was stupid. That led to the cycle of underachievement.

What I did was to help Mary to articulate her thoughts, feelings, and opinions to her parents. Once they understood her needs, they and she together could work on ways to help Mary manage her stress.

After a year of remedial school work and several months of therapy, Mary called to tell me that she had made the honor roll. She was very proud, hardly sounding like the teen who'd been in such a deep crisis just the year before. As it turned out, that crisis had proven to be an opportunity for Mary and her parents strengthen and grow as a family.

Serious depression is treatable but is difficult to diagnose. The symptoms sometimes may be mistaken for Attention-Deficit Hyperactivity Disorder (ADHD).

Among teens, depression is often disguised in smoking, drinking, or drug use.

It's important that you look out for serious depression and doubly important that you heed the great deal of research that shows that the more family-like connections a person has, the more inoculated against depression they are.

Lessons Learned

As we've seen, stress can come from many sources. It can worsen if your teen gets into serious problems like teen pregnancy, drug or alcohol abuse, and gangs. Fortunately, most teens make it through adolescence without major problems, but it's important that you know what to look for and work to stay connected.

Occasional challenges, both physical and psychological, are not unhealthy. So you shouldn't try to make everything in life stress-free. Instead, try to develop the ability to relax during day-to-day activities and during challenging occurrences.

Again, look first at your own stress level. Do all you can to live a balanced life and set the right example for your teens. Teens need to know every day that their parents care about them; so, tell them and show them even if they're "stressed" or "weirded out."

As with so many aspects of raising a teen, you will need to walk a narrow line between giving him or her independence while still finding ways to be supportive and spend time together. Do what you can to show them they can talk to you. Be candid about your frustrations as well as your successes. Learn all you can and do all you can to reduce their stress. And don't expect them to be superhuman, just human.

It all comes down to focus and control. Try to help your teen focus on what's really important and to control what he or she can without sweating the rest. For any of us, that's easier said than done. But for your teen it's especially important that you try.

chapter 10

Making Character Count

Character, I think, is a lot like chili con carne. Everyone has his or her own idea about the best ingredients. And while reasonable people can disagree about what should go into the cooking pot, everybody *knows* what really good chili tastes like when it's done.

It's the same with character: We all think we know what virtues give a person strength and integrity, and those virtues may vary widely. But we all know and admire a person of impeccable character when we see one.

So trying to list the components of character may be a little like trying to describe the best place to vacation, or the best things to eat, or the most pleasant things to do on a sunny, summer afternoon; it all depends on who's making the list.

For whatever it's worth, here is my list of what constitutes character—*Responsibility, Respect, Resilience, Humility, Kindness,* and *Honesty.* In this chapter I'm going to detail what I think those mean and why they're important for you to try to instill in your teens. And, of course, I'll give you suggestions on just how to do that.

Be a Parent, Not a Pushover

What is character?

"Character," the Greek philosopher Heraclitus said, "is destiny." And if we wish to have our teens become fulfilled and contributing adults we must instill character in them. But what do we mean by character?

We don't mean a person's eccentricity, as suggested by the phrase, "He's *such* a character." Instead, we mean character in its moral sense, the capacity to act in a way that reveals an inner set of moral values.

So there are really two faces of moral character: what we believe (our values) and what we do. In those with the finest character, the two faces are as one. There's no slippage between our values and our actions.

Further, to be a person of real character, one needs to have *all* the elements, not just some. If a person were, for instance, kind, responsible, and respectful . . . but also dishonest or lacking the resilience to keep going when times got tough, he or she wouldn't be said to have much character. Similarly, character shouldn't stop at social or political borders. It wouldn't be in good character to, say, be kind, responsible, and respectful just to one's family (or just to one's own gender, race, or nation) and be less than that to all others.

So true character isn't like a hat that a person takes on or off, depending on whom he or she is with. And it's not some splendid but isolated virtue that the holder fervently espouses when he's alone with his thoughts but jettisons when faced with a real-life situation. Instead, it's *the practice of a person's essential core values with everyone.*

No. 1 teacher

And you, the parent, are the No.1 teacher of character to your teen at a time when he or she really *needs* to be taught. Because at the heart of all teenage problems are the fundamental questions each of us wrestles with as young people:

Who am I?
And how do I relate to the world?

Many people—even as adults—never get very clear answers to those questions. As a result, they bounce from crisis to crisis, dealing with symptoms but not issues, operating from their gut instead of their head.

But if you can build character in your kid, that will go a long way toward answering those two key questions with a clarity that most people lack. Having solid answers will help immensely to smooth your teen's path through life.

To do a good job of instilling character means *you* are going to need to be strong. You probably will need to be tougher with your teen than you're used to being—and tougher on yourself, too. You may need to remind yourself that you're the adult, that you have the superior judgment, that you *can* work through any problems the two of you face.

You can't yield, for instance, to the very human temptation of asserting control one week and giving it back the next, or setting limits and then shrugging off any discipline when they're exceeded. Sometimes you must let teens experience the results of their own behavior and discourage them from thinking Mom or Dad will always ride to the rescue. None of this is easy. But it's the capstone, the culmination of much of what we've discussed in this book.

The role of peer pressure

I said you were the No. 1 teacher. But you're not the only teacher. The teen's friends and associates, his or her peers, also play a big role.

The very idea of peer pressure, laden with negative images of leather-clad gangs and forbidden pleasures, gives many parents sweaty palms. After all, what if their teen starts following the crowd—and maybe a bad crowd at that—instead of hewing to the parental line?

And, indeed, this could be a concern. But if you've been doing the other things you should—communicating well, spending time with your teen, setting a good example, and giving love and direction—you shouldn't have too much to fear.

In fact, peer influence also can be positive and instructive because it teaches kids how to get along in the world. Interacting with peer groups is about learning to fit in. More often than not, sociologists believe, peers reinforce family values. In part, it's peer pressure that keeps teens going to 4-H, singing in the church choir, or playing on sports teams.

Truth is, peer groups are not, as some parents see them, a united front of dangerous influences. Any teen interacts with many different peer groups with varying values and norms. The "jocks" at school may have one set of values while the more cerebral kids another and the kids who ride the school bus yet another. While some of these may have the potential to encourage problem behaviors, it's not a conspiracy, and it's probably nothing that your own family values, if strong, can't counteract.

Yes, there's risk. Teens through their peer groups do take their first big steps away from the family. And in doing so, the teen may begin to question adult standards and the need for parental guidance. Clearly, a peer group provides the teen a source of affection, sympathy, and understanding. But if the teen also is getting those things at home, it's doubtful the peer group will lead him or her too far astray.

Take, for instance, smoking and drinking. Teen smoking and drinking do not occur in a vacuum, new research shows. Both parents and peers may promote—*or* discourage—substance abuse among teens, according to a study of more than 4,500 Maryland junior high schoolers.

The research by the National Institute of Child Health and Human Development, found that girls and boys with friends who smoke and drank were more likely to do so themselves. But parents also appeared to influence teen smoking and drinking.

"Teens who perceived that their parents like them, respect them, take them seriously, listen to them and give reasons for rules and decision that involve them were less likely to smoke and drink," said Bruce Simons-Morton, the study's lead author.

Teens are more likely to experiment with alcohol and tobacco if their parents don't establish clear expectations, don't make an effort to keep informed about their teen's life, and don't show respect and regard for the teen, Simons-Morton added.

Be a Parent, Not a Pushover

Thus, it seems clear to me, that a strong one-on-one connection with a responsible, loving adult, whether a parent, teacher or coach, is a more powerful influence than are peers. My advice: Be the best parent you can be, and don't overly worry about the effect of peer groups on your teen.

Now, let's look in more detail at the character traits and what's involved in trying to get our teens to buy into them.

Responsibility

Do you seem to always be dashing off to school because your teenager forgot his lunch or her purse? Or left her homework in the computer printer? Or didn't take his gym bag despite this being a P.E. day?

If so, you may be encouraging irresponsibility. You may be failing to make clear to your teen one of life's major lessons: Bad behavior produces bad results.

Sure, everybody has an odd bad day when they forget something or otherwise act in a way that's just plain dumb. But I'm talking about people—teenagers or adults—whom you just can't trust because of their chronic inattention, their poor work habits, their generally sloppy approach to both people and tasks. These are the people you don't call when something important needs to be done.

You probably know people like that at work or in your family. Maybe they procrastinate or are chronically late. Perhaps they're quick to promise but slow to perform. They may lack follow-through or are satisfied with a mediocre effort on any job. All this takes a toll on their effectiveness. They may be kind and lovely people, but they are irresponsible. Being kind and lovely is nice, but it's not enough to make them responsible.

You don't want your teenager to grow into an adult like that. But you may be encouraging that if you continually bail him or her out of self-created jams.

One of the first tasks under the job description of parent is helping your child become a responsible adult. Do so, and he or she will fare much better in the world.

So, what can you do?

For starters, make sure you're responsible

Did you recognize yourself in the above description of an irresponsible person? How's your follow-through? Your punctuality? Your attention to detail? If those are not so good, you might want to start work on them right now, not just for your sake but for your teen's, too.

Go easy on the lectures

Responsibility is a lot like love; it's better demonstrated that talked about. You can't very well lecture someone about how to love better. But you can show them how being loved feels. Similarly, a child must learn responsibility by doing and finding out the results of his behavior.

Trust your teen to make mistakes

Or, to put in another way, encourage him or her to make choices and live with the consequences. This is tough because we don't want our kids to make the mistakes we did. And sometimes we feel guilty for not spending more time with the teen, so we compensate by over-protecting them. But in neither case are we doing them much of a favor.

True, there are some high-risk behaviors you just don't want them experiencing, such as riding in a car with someone who's been drinking, or being involved in a risky or abusive sexual situation.

But for most choices—let's say, deciding between going to a dance or doing his homework—there's a wider safety net, and you should err on the side of letting the kid choose. In fact, whenever possible, you should insist on having the teen make the choice and refuse to make it for him. This is a small start toward helping your teen grow up and become a good decision maker.

He or she may do poorly on the homework, or even do poorly in the class, by deciding instead to go to the dance. But in the long run, getting a poor grade may be a small price to pay for a valuable lesson.

Got a kid who can't seem to get up in time for school? Two suggestions: (1) Get her a clock, and (2) Make it her responsibility from here on out. If you allow the teen to make this *your* problem and your responsibility to get her up, you're potentially creating a monster by rewarding bad behavior. And if you nag her about getting up and remind her repeatedly about the time, you're giving her a kind of attention that may be counterproductive.

Instead, try this: Be sure the kid has a clock and give her full responsibility for getting herself up and dressed in time. Don't nag her at all. If she does arise in time, you'll be there to fix breakfast and enjoy it with her. If she doesn't, she makes her own breakfast or skips it. Left to her own devices, she may even be late for school but that can be instructional, too.

Whatever the result, she will know that the rules are for real. And that it's up to her to take responsibility for her own actions.

Never call your teen "irresponsible"

You may think that on occasion, but don't throw around that label carelessly. It can become a self-fulfilling prophecy. If the teen, for example, forgets that he promised to help a neighbor fix a fence and instead goes to the movies, don't lash out at him; he probably feels bad enough already. Instead, help him figure out how he can make it up to the neighbor. That's a much more positive approach.

Don't do your teen's homework

It's surprising how many parents get caught in the trap of doing the teen's out-of-class assignments with them or for them. Homework is the student's responsibility, not yours. Sure, he or she may need some help now and then. But you shouldn't be sitting down with your teen night after night to work, say, on his math. Nor should you need to nag him to tackle his assignments. You might want to help him or her set up a schedule and budget his time. But regardless of how much you want him to succeed, you're sending the wrong message if you routinely do the work. The higher grade is not worth it if the lesson of responsibility is lost along the way.

Be a Parent, Not a Pushover

Don't be a bottomless "bank"

Teens need to learn not to spend more money than they have. Discourage your teen from thinking it's O.K. to borrow from you when he wants something badly, then pay you back when he gets more money. For one thing, he probably won't pay you back. For another, you're encouraging fiscal irresponsibility, a scourge that already infects all too many adults.

Instead, urge him to spend only what he has, and even to save some of that. Discuss with him how you manage your money and what kinds of savings programs and investment plans people use.

You may even *want* him to have those new skis or that nifty jacket before he has the money. But if you give him the dough, he won't appreciate the item as much as if he'd earned it on his own. Give him the money and you cheat him out of the learning experience that in the long run will be much more helpful than having the new skis or jacket now.

Respect

You walk in the door after work, and young Frederick, hunched over his Gameboy, can't even come up with a muted "Hello, Dad" in response to your greeting. Instead, he silently focuses on his video game with the intensity of a scientist scrutinizing a strand of DNA. Or maybe he's staring at MTV as if it's the last television show ever to be broadcast.

You walk over to him and put your hand on his shoulder. "I said, 'Hello, Fred.' Did you hear me?"

"Oh, yeah. Hello. Or . . . whatever."

You wonder: Whatever happened to the Fifth Commandment, "Honor Thy Parents"?

The truth is, children need to learn gratitude. One likely object of their gratitude ought to be their parents. So maybe the kid thinks the folks are not the greatest parents in the world. That wouldn't be an unprecedented thought. But still Mom and Dad deserve and desire some respect.

Teens who respect their parents are going to respect other authority figures, too. And that's not a bad habit for them to get into. Because even if authority figures (perhaps you included) have feet of clay clear up to their knees, society is built in no small measure on respect for authority, whether in school, on the job, or in the family.

How do you encourage respect? Well, for starters, you can't wait until the kid is a teen before bringing up the "R" word. Start at a young age to get the child in the habit of speaking and acting respectfully.

How?

Expect proper salutations

Asking your children to politely address elders (other than parents or close relatives)—for example, as "Mr.," "Mrs.," "Ma'm," and "Sir"—may seem old-fashioned, but it doesn't seem to me to be requesting too much. Requiring that parents and close relatives be greeted when they arrive and be routinely called by their title ("Mom" and "Dad," for instance, and "Aunt Hope" and "Uncle Jim") seems reasonable as well.

Be a Parent, Not a Pushover

If you wait until your kid is a teen is start this habit, it's probably going to seem degrading to him or her. If you start them early, it'll just be the natural thing to do.

As always, it's best to model the behavior you seek. When your spouse comes home, do you drop what you're doing for at least a short time and greet him or her warmly?

Make serving others a part of life

Doing little things—bringing water to someone who looks hot and thirsty, for example, or passing the sweet potatoes before taking some yourself, or being exceptionally quiet when someone is napping—is another way to show respect.

Again, these are small habits, but with big impacts. Such small kindnesses amount to a social lubricant, helping to put others at ease and to feel valued as individuals. Graciousness is never out of style, even for young people.

Do you make it a point to do little things for your spouse, letting him or her read the paper first, for instance, or putting out a bowl of his or her favorite snack, or drawing a warm bath for your husband or wife after a hard day? If you do, young eyes will be watching.

Whatever you do, don't be so intent on serving your kids that you unwittingly send the message that *they* are here to be waited on and not to serve others. Nor, of course, do you want them to feel like "go-fers." But this is a wide road: You can ask for some show of selflessness on their part without being overly demanding.

Stress appreciation

Honest gratitude is greatly under-appreciated. Teach your kids to express their thanks when you, or someone else, goes out of their way to help them. And remember to thank your teen when he does something out of the ordinary for you or for the family.

Don't disrespect your spouse, ex-spouse, or your parents

As I've said several times elsewhere in this book, try to keep your anger or your marital differences as private as possible. Do the same when discussing your parents or in-laws. That will help inculcate respect in your children and your teens.

Don't allow arguing to go on

Discussing a difference of opinion is one thing, but arguing is another. Don't let teens harangue you, or you them. If they disagree, for example, with your repeated requests for them to make their bed, just tell them: "Please make your bed now. All the other beds in the house are made by whomever sleeps in them. So, please, do yours now. If you think that's an unfair request, we can talk it over later."

Don't be wishy-washy

It's hard for a teen to respect a parent who runs hot and cold on any given issue. Be firm about what you expect from your kids and what the rules are. Be open to discussing possible changes in the rules if the teen can calmly show the need and logic for that. But don't change them just because the teen

crinkles his or her nose at the idea of cutting the grass or setting the table or whatever else he is asked to do.

❧

By requiring respect from our teens, we're not just feeding
parental egos. We're helping build in the teens the character
that will serve them well throughout their lives.

But, as in all matters pertaining to child-raising, you need
to *show*, not just tell, how it's done. If you want your teens to
respect you and other adults, you've got to demonstrate respect in word and deed. When you make a promise, keep it.
When you claim moral standards, live by them. And when
you desire to be surrounded by graciousness, be yourself un-
failingly thoughtful, appreciative, and refined in speech and
manner.

Resilience

Resilience is the ability to bounce back, to keep on course despite disappointments and setbacks. It's a sign of emotional
health. I suppose it might also be called "courage."

Whatever it's called, if a kid knows for sure that you're on
his or her side, that's a great advantage in developing resilience. If he knows you'll be there for him to talk to and help
solve his problems, he's likely to develop a sense of mastery of
his own life.

Sure, the resilient teen will still get frustrated by mistakes
or difficult situations. But deep down, he'll have the feeling
that they won't last forever and, moreover, that he can learn
from them.

Many studies show the primary factor in being resilient is having caring and supporting relationships within and outside the family. Other factors associated with resilience include many of the suggestions made elsewhere in this book, such as the ability of the teen to make realistic plans, possess a positive self-image, develop communication skills, and manage strong feelings and impulses.

Many of the violent kids we read about, such as those who shoot up schools, are reported to be terribly isolated, and when you're terribly isolated, life sometimes seems impossible. Robert Brooks and Sam Goldstein, in their book *Raising Resilient Children*, stress the need for a linchpin relationship between a child and at least one parent, or a parental figure (for instance, a teacher or a coach), someone with whom the kid can identify and from whom he can gather strength.

Thus, resilience is not a trait that we're born with or without. It's a skill and a mindset, something that can be learned. In fact, resilience, according to the American Psychological Association, can be learned by most anyone. And there's no one way, no optimum strategy, for a person seeking to be resilient. Instead, resilience is a combination of behaviors, thoughts, and actions.

How can you help your teen develop a personal strategy for increasing resilience?

Spend lots of time with the teen

Obviously, this can't be overstated. Everything we know suggests that the presence of even one caring adult can positively affect a teen's life.

Be a Parent, Not a Pushover

Yet research suggests too many parents don't make the effort. A Temple University study of 20,000 high school students found that about 30% of parents were significantly uninvolved in their kids' lives and couldn't describe how the youths spent their time or who their friends were.

You've *got* to make this commitment if you want your kid to be able to best weather life's storms. Sure, your job is important. And your spouse's needs are, too. And maybe even your golf game or your bridge club cries out for attention. But you must find time in there—*lots* of time—for your teenager, or you're inviting big problems for him or her and, ultimately, for you.

Find and develop the teen's areas of competence

It's imperative that everyone—perhaps especially teenagers—know they are good at *some*thing. Those "islands of competence," as Brooks calls them, are the source of needed self-confidence.

Your teen stinks at sports and isn't much better at his schoolwork? O.K., what does he like to do? Maybe he's a latent artist, or is good with plants, or just is a kind and generous person who everyone enjoys being around. Help him find that skill or attribute, whatever it is. Call attention to it over and over, and support your teen's pursuit of it.

Sometimes we parents have such a reflexive tendency to stamp out bad behavior that we overlook the good. We chide our kids for not getting a good grade in chemistry or for not making the basketball team, but we overlook their virtuosity on a skateboard or their marvelous singing voice or their writing skill. Help them discover—and polish—those hidden diamonds.

Encourage the teen to make connections

Isolation is the arch-enemy of resilience. So do what you can to encourage your teen to be active in civic groups, faith-based organizations, school clubs, or other organizations. Because assisting others in their time of need can also help the helper, urge the teen to donate time and effort to the less fortunate.

Try to provide some perspective

Give the teen the benefit of your years and your insight by helping him or her to take a longer view. Whatever the crisis, show him that it's probably not insurmountable. Help him to accept change as a part of living and to look beyond the present to how future circumstances may be better. Encourage him to visualize what he wants rather than worrying about what he fears.

Help pinpoint the learning opportunities in misfortune

"Many are the uses of adversity," Shakespeare told us, and who among us hasn't gotten stronger as a result of this crisis or that? All adults know that people grow as a result of their struggle with loss. But that may be a fresh concept for a 16-year-old.

Be a Parent, Not a Pushover

Get the teen to pay attention to his or her own needs

Teens, like the rest of us, need the flexibility and balance that come from getting enough rest and exercise and taking some time out for ourselves. It's easy in the hectic teenage world to become overtaxed. But you can nudge them toward taking better care of themselves.

☙

Of course, being resilient doesn't mean a person won't suffer difficulty or distress. It just means he or she will handle it better. So do what you can to help build your teen's resiliency by talking to and supporting him or her. Make him feel special and appreciated. Volunteer your more long-term perspective on your teen's problems and encourage him to recognize his talents and strong points.

Humility

When I say humility, I don't mean weakness or meekness. I mean a lack of arrogance. I mean the sense of being so comfortable with who you are that you can see others as equals, not competitors or subordinates. That's a big order, but it is, to my mind, a key component of character.

When I reflect on humility, I think of a most remarkable man in my city who started with nothing, the son of a poor immigrant fruit peddler. But the son made a fortune in banking and, more important, has made a very full life. Though in his 80s now, he possesses the spirit of a teenager. And his secret, I believe, is humility.

Not only a business success, he's also been an aviator, an artist, a writer, and has mastered a few other avocations. His secret: He sees himself as a student and everyone as his teacher. That's how he engages life.

When the gardener comes to tend to his lawn, this man talks to him at length about the plants and their habits. When he hired an editor to help him with his memoirs, he hungered to learn the ins and outs of word processing. When he studied sculpture, he sought and got another education in raw materials and form.

He's the youngest octogenarian I've ever met. He's also an object lesson in humility because he could have begun with the premise that he's a rich, experienced banker and you're merely a gardener . . . or a writer . . . or a lowly teacher of sculpture. But instead he plunged in as an equal and emerged the better for it.

That's what humility amounts to: Not thinking you're a nobody, but thinking you have inner strengths that can be sharpened by recognizing the potential greatness in others. Only the humble person can acknowledge the bigness in others. A big, strong teenage football player who is humble knows he has a skill, but he also knows that other kids are good at math, science, and history. It's the small-minded one who becomes the bully or puts people down.

How can you inculcate this view?

Teach teens to ask questions, not make declarations

This goes hand in hand with Respect. Asking questions is such a softer, more gracious way of starting a dialogue than just announcing a foregone conclusion.

It also is far more likely to get results.

Be a Parent, Not a Pushover

Words are deeds. For example, consider if your teen said:

Declaration: *I just won't do the dishes any more.*
Question: *Is it possible that someone else could do the dishes?*

The former probably sets your teeth to grinding. (You think, *Uh oh, here we go again! Another fight in the making.*) But the latter, especially if spoken in a pleasant tone of voice, suggests reason and the possibility of options. (You conclude, *She has a problem with doing the dishes. Let's find out what it is. Maybe it's legitimate and perhaps there's a way to work around it.*)

Thus, a teen with humility *asks* his or her parents, doesn't *tell* them. Just by a slight change of words, the kid subtly acknowledges the experience, knowledge, and maturity of his elders.

If you want your teens to use words that show respect for adults, you want to start as early as possible when they're children. But if not, start now to wean them from an arrogant and "me-centered" vocabulary. You'll be helping to build humility.

Encourage them to admit errors or shortcomings

This is a lesson we all could learn, but the humble person always keeps in mind the possibility that he or she could be wrong or could do better.

Your 17-year-old, for example, didn't make the starting team in hockey, and he's very upset with the coach who said his stick handling "needed work." Your kid fumes, *Why, that coach is so stupid that he doesn't know good stick handling when he sees it! I'm so mad I'm never going to go on the ice again. I'll quit. That'll show him!*

Actually, quitting wouldn't show the coach anything except that he made a good choice in choosing his starters. Perhaps the coach is a poor one, but maybe, just maybe, he knows what he's talking about.

If you want your son to gain some humility, you'll raise that possibility. And you might also suggest he go back to the coach and politely ask for some specifics on what he could do to improve. You may also want to suggest that the boy get a second opinion from another coach or expert. When that's done, perhaps you could help him plan his next move: Improve his hockey game, or maybe choose another sport.

Demonstrate your own humility

How? The simplest, most direct way possible: By not being arrogant with your teen.

You need to give respect before you can get it. So, in short, don't get swept away with your parental authority. Yes, you need to make rules, but you don't need to make them in a vacuum without talking to your teen and others, without explaining their reason for being, without being able to enforce them in an atmosphere of calm and love.

If the only way you can get a teen to listen is by yelling, then you're not modeling humility. If "*How dare you defy me!*" is your idea of dialogue, then you're seriously on the wrong track. Instead, try to operate in a way that will preserve the kid's dignity—and your own.

Be a Parent, Not a Pushover

Be open to the possibility that you and/or your teen may need professional help

It takes humility to admit that your problems need the attention of a therapist. Teenage boys, particularly, are resistant to the idea that outside intervention will help. But if you and your teen have intractable problems and just can't seem to talk about them and/or serious drug or alcohol abuse exists, you need to ask for assistance.

Selecting a therapist for a child is a highly personal matter. You probably will need to interview more than one to get a sense of who will interact best with the teen and the parent(s). First, you might want to check with your health-insurance carrier for any limitations. Then talk to family members and friends for their recommendations. Your physician or pastor might also be a source of referrals, and you can also look in the phone book for a listing of the local mental health association or community mental health center.

Kindness

In a world where violence, cruelty, and incivility reign, does kindness count? Yes, because however scarce it may sometimes seem, kindness is the mark of a mature man or woman. Caring and compassion for others may not be a staple of TV reality shows or even of reality itself, but it's what makes a human being human.

It's important for your teen's character that you send him or her signals about how deeply you feel about his or her behavior, whether good or bad, toward others. Raising kids to be kind involves more than getting them to say "please" and "thank you." It means helping them to rise above their own needs and wants in a society that peppers us with just the opposite message.

So you want to praise teens when they're exceptionally kind and thoughtful. And when they are unkind, you should be clear about that, too. Condemn the act, not the teen. Say *Wouldn't it have been a kind thing to do to help that poor man who stumbled while crossing the street?* not, *You're a terrible person for not helping him out.*

Helping teens become givers, not just takers, is not an easy job, but it's do-able.

What are some of the ways?

Mirror what you wish them to become

This is hardly news to you by now, but the more your kids see you as consistently caring and compassionate, the more they are likely to be the same. Not everyone, of course, has the skill or energy to devote days to helping out at the hospice or baking sheet cakes for the 4-H group or making other big-caliber contributions in time or money.

But small acts of compassion are just as important, maybe more so in aggregate. Saving a stray pet from euthanasia, for instance, or helping out a homeless person, doing a favor for someone who's sick, or speaking up on behalf of one who's being teased or tormented, these acts speak volumes.

Start a compassionate cycle in the home

Youngsters should be trained at an early age to be aware of who needs help in the family. Does Grandpa need his cane or could Dad use a hand in the garden? Could the teen help Mom fold those towels or bring in the wash? Can we be proactive in doing things for family members and friends before we're even asked? If the kid sees and acts on such opportunities, praise him or her profusely, not for the act of helping so much as for the sensitivity shown.

Reinforce kindness as much as accomplishment

You make much out of an improved grade in algebra, as well you should. But do you get as enthused when your teen goes out of his way to help a disadvantaged person or volunteers at the senior citizens' home? Do you applaud peacemaking as much as verbal sparring? Do you cheer as loudly for acts of good sportsmanship as for victory?

Watch media consumption

Can watching too much of what's on television, movies, and video games make your teen hard and uncaring? Without a doubt, I think. So what to do?

Well, you can't hope to block all such influences, but you can seek to dilute or counteract them. For example, give your teens books that promote kindness and compassion. Recommend movies or TV shows that glorify humanity, not violence. Educate your youngsters about famous people you admire for the altruistic deeds they've done.

Encourage involvement

Suggest organized ways for your teens to get engaged in the community. One study found that teenagers who were involved in helping others felt very positive about their lives and were hopeful about their own futures. Many volunteer organizations and churches have special programs for young people.

Another idea: Go to www.actsofkindness.org, the site for the Random Acts of Kindness Foundation. Founded in 1995, the foundation provides ideas, lesson plans, projects, teacher's guides, and other resources for spreading kindness—all for free.

None of these approaches will work in the absence of a culture of caring between you and the teen, or an absence of genuine loving-kindness in the home.

Honesty

The person of good character not only does not steal or cheat, he or she also is honest with himself and others. This is not a trait that we see a lot, but it is one worth inculcating in your teen if, for no other reason, than it will make him or her stand out.

But even a better reason is that it'll help build your relationship with your kid. If your teen thinks you're a truth teller, someone who is on the level and can be leveled with, he or she is going to be more honest with you.

What do we mean by "honesty?" We mean not being a thief or a cheater, of course, but also being as forthright, as open, as possible, not secretive or shifty in either thought or action. So much of our society—or any society, I suppose—is built on lying or dissembling or putting the best face on a situation. As a result, role models are in short supply. But *you* can be one. In fact, it's crucial that you do. The downsides of being dishonest are severe and are everywhere visible.

A web of dishonesty

Many parents start out weaving a web of dishonesty with their kids. First, there's the Tooth Fairy, the Easter Bunny, and Santa Claus. Later, when the kids are still small, there's the Stork.

Then when they're older and after they've given up on the idea of gifts or babies being brought by anthropomorphic creatures or saintly old gentlemen, there's probably dishonesty of a different sort: the parental failure to talk about sex and drugs or to be honest about the family's fortunes. (This leads to other myths: perhaps including the one that says all family members are mentally and financially healthy. Or, that love is the predominant emotion in the home. Or, that alcohol is used there merely as a social lubricant, not a medication.)

Probably also not talked about is life's final chapter in general, and specifically, why everyone's so hush-hush about the debilitating disease that claimed Aunt Evelyn. Maybe *"We just don't discuss it!"* becomes a family mantra, whether the subject is a controversial branch of the family tree, why Mom and Dad don't seem to be getting along, or why don't we hear anymore from Cousin Ed, who lives faraway in a town known for its state prison.

These lies or omissions are probably not big-caliber items in and of themselves. But they help create an unspoken policy of deceit and dissembling that can come to suffocate the truth. Prevaricating, not being honest, becomes the family's stock in trade. After a while, everybody in the household becomes really good at lying or, at least, being mute about the truth.

But here's the bottom line: If you hide things from your teens, if you teach them that not speaking the truth is different from telling a lie, they're probably going to do the same with you and others.

> Parent: *Where did you go last night?*
> Teen: *Just out.*
> Parent: *With whom?*
> Teen: *Just some kids.*
> Parent: *What did you do?*
> Teen *Hung out.*
> Parent: *How 'bout tonight? What's up?*
> Teen: *Same.*

Sound familiar? Maybe it's a chorus you helped create. Think about that.

Specific steps

Meanwhile, what specific steps can you take to try to build honesty in your teen?

Express shock—in word and action—at all thievery

You heard the old joke about the school principal who calls the father in to tell him that his son has been stealing pens from the school? The father is outraged. "I can't understand why he would do such a thing. He has plenty of pens. I bring boxes and boxes of them home from the office!"

Be a Parent, Not a Pushover

Society has suffered from time immemorial from cheating and stealing. That probably isn't going to change. (In fact, it may be getting worse. A survey of 12,000 high school students by the Josephson Institute of Ethics found that students who admitted to cheating on an exam at least once in the prior year jumped from 61% in 1992 to 74% a decade later; the number who shoplifted in the previous year rose from 31% to 38% over the same period.)

But that doesn't mean you need to encourage or condone it in your family. Not doing so, of course, means setting the example.

Do you give lip service to honesty but, deep down, believe that if everybody does something, it's not really bad? Do you return change when a clerk gives you too much back? Report *all* your income to the IRS? Fib about a kid's age to get a cheaper admission price to a movie or theme park? Munch on some grapes you pull off a bunch at the supermarket and then not buy them?

If we really want to give our children and teens a higher standard of honesty, such small, everyday lessons will count for something.

Be forthright about sharing

Kids are pretty astute about recognizing what parents hide from them or when they disguise the truth. No, you don't need to tell your teens about every personal detail of your past or present life; you've got to use good judgment. But you can probably share more than you do.

If the household is having money problems, you can tell the teen the scope and reasons for the dilemma, if not the precise dollars and cents. If there's a crisis involving a parent's job or a proposed relocation, for instance, the kid is going to be affected sooner or later; you might as well be upfront. Or if a beloved grandparent is gravely ill, you probably should go ahead and say it's ovarian cancer or lymphoma or whatever, because the kid is going to pick up on your grim mood in any event. That we all die is no secret, even to the most sheltered teen; so you can afford to be frank.

You should share such information because (1) it's the honest thing to do; and (2) if you don't, the teen is going to take your silence or your euphemism as a condemnation of him or her. *They're not sharing because they don't think I'm mature enough to handle it*, the teen will think.

Then there's a third reason you should share: Being honest with teens allows them to feel more comfortable talking about themselves. If you let them know, for instance, that you did your share of experimenting when you were their age, perhaps you'll raise the level of honesty about sex and drugs. Of course, the bad news is that you won't appear like an infallible authority anymore. Admitting your flaws and mistakes may mean you forfeit your right to preach. But wouldn't that be worth it to hear about some issues you otherwise wouldn't have?

When we're honest, the subject, whatever it may be, is brought above board. It's easier then for teens to ask questions. And when we hear their questions, we can get a sense of their fears and feelings. And how are we going to help them if we don't know their fears and feelings? How are they going to learn to handle their own painful feelings if all such thoughts are suppressed?

By speaking honestly and sensitively about the death of a family member, for example, you can model compassion and coping. You can show the teen that it's possible to remain calm even in the face of terrible news. Or by talking about your own indiscretions, you can send the signal that candor, not shame or secrecy, is the order of the day.

Insist they be honest with you

If you're honest with your teen on subjects large and small, it's reasonable to ask they treat you similarly.

A lot of how successful this will be, though, will depend on the nature of your relationship.

So this may take some time. You may need to build up to this point, to prove that you're worthy of their "confessions." How? One, by not getting upset if they tell you something you don't want to hear. Two, by showing, if need be, that you can be discreet. Fear of being teased or yelled at or harassed (if not by you, by your spouse, a sibling, or other teens) is a major impediment to honesty among teens.

So if your daughter tells you she and her friends drank a lot of beer, then went swimming naked in the quarry with a bunch of boys, are you going to flip out and imagine the worst? Are you going to be condemning, or consoling?

Or, say, your son admits to some minor vandalizing in the park. Are you going to freak out and immediately call the authorities, vowing to send the kid "to jail, if necessary"? Or are you going to, first, try to calmly get to the bottom of this?

What, exactly, did he do and why? Can we undo the damage? How can we keep from having this happen again?

In other words, you're going to have to earn your teen's respect. You're going to have to show that you're a worthy repository for honesty.

Insist they be honest with others

Don't participate in the often elaborate excuses and "cover stories" that teens sometimes feel compelled to fabricate as a result of peer pressure.

Maybe your daughter asks you to help her come up with a phony story about why she wants to room with one of her high school friends in the college dorm but to reject another. If she chooses Friend A, Friend B and her group will think less of her. As a result, she thinks she'll lose some advantage that could accrue from being a part of that circle of friends.

But instead of helping her lie, explore her motivations and desired outcomes. And then help her come up with the most honest explanation that you both hope will satisfy all concerned. But if it doesn't, prepare her to accept the consequences.

Lessons Learned

"There is nothing more influential, more determinant in a child's life than the moral power of a quiet example," wrote William Bennett in *The Book of Virtues*. And so it is with all phases of building character in your teen.

You need to be clear about your values. You need to tell your children where you stand on important personal issues.

Be a Parent, Not a Pushover

And you need to capitalize on any teachable moment that presents itself as a chance to show your commitment to Responsibility, Respect, Resilience, Humility, Kindness, and Honesty.

Set clear expectations and hold your teens accountable for their actions. Show respect for the people around you and resolve your differences in peaceful ways that send your kids a powerful message about respect.

Do all you can to help your teens discover and underscore their areas of competence. Silently demonstrate humility by not being arrogant with your teen, and put caring and concern for others at the top of your agenda. And refuse to cover for your kids and make excuses for their inappropriate behavior.

Remember, teens don't need another buddy who agrees with them on everything. They need a parent who cares enough to set and enforce appropriate limits and who will be a model to help them learn and grow. "In the last analysis," writes Stephen Covey, "what we are communicates far more eloquently than anything we say or do."

Trust Yourself to Be the Best Parent You Can Be

*P*arents too often believe that every interaction with their teen is fraught with grave psychological repercussions. Embrace the kid too much, and he will become a softy, dependent and clingy. But keep him at arm's length and he'll feel unloved—and that, parents feel sure, can lead to all sorts of anti-social behavior, up to and including homicidal rage.

So what do today's Moms and Dads do? Sometimes almost nothing. Semi-paralyzed with fear over small issues that parents a generation or two ago would have settled in a heartbeat, modern parents too often waffle. They don't set limits. Or if they do, they go slack when the time comes to enforce them. Or they enforce some rules sometimes and others not at all. As a result, their kids are largely adrift. When that happens, teens look for structure elsewhere. And that elsewhere may be something unsavory, such as drugs, gangs, or crime.

In truth, teenage psyches aren't so fragile that we can't be parents who set rules and set good examples. Not only should we make rules, our kids actually *want* us to. And endeavoring to be good role models will not only aid our kids, it'll help us, too.

In this book I've talked about a lot of issues and have given perhaps hundreds of specific bits of advice. Because I want those suggestions to be helpful and not overwhelming, I'm going to add here a coda, a short afterthought that sort of sums things up: *Be the best person you can be, then trust yourself to be a good parent.*

Sometimes I find that Moms and Dads have lost all confidence in themselves as parents. They've heard so many horror stories from other Moms and Dads or read so many articles or heard so many lectures about parenting that it's as if they've gotten to the middle of a frozen lake and in whichever direction they step they hear an ominous creaking sound. So how do they react? By standing absolutely still and hoping the ice doesn't thaw even more. That's not a very good strategy for making it across this icy lake we call parenting.

Parenting *is* a tough job. But it's not, as the saying has it, rocket science. You don't have to be brilliant at it, just adequate. There are almost 30 million American teenagers, and most of them have decent parents and become decent adults, even if there are a few bumps along the way.

So do heed my advice and trust yourself to make a good effort. Be tough but fair. And work hard at being a good person yourself. That's all that's required in most cases to raise pretty worthwhile kids.

A thinking problem

I'm a psychologist, and so of course I've spent a lot of time trying to figure out the whys and wherefores of human behavior. But I also think we can over-analyze. In many parent-teen conflicts, what's at issue is not a psychological problem as much as a thinking problem. Parents need to do more clear thinking and less fretting about the purported emotional toll of every twist and turn of their teen's journey to adulthood.

Specifically, you need to ask yourself:

- *Am I spending as much time as possible with my kid?* If not, how can I ratchet up that interaction?
- *Am I setting clear, reasonable rules and enforcing them?* Sure, I need to explain the reasons for the rules, but I don't need to apologize for them; I am the parent, after all.
- *Am I modeling the behavior I'd like my teen to mirror?* All the rules and lofty language in the world won't make much difference if you don't embody the behavior you seek in the child.
- *Am I perceiving—and reinforcing—my teen's uniqueness?* In other words, do I really, *really* love this kid—and show it?

I said this earlier but I can't over-emphasize: If there is just one thing you should and must do, it's spend more time with your kid. Not being with them is the root of most of the problems we've discussed. *Spend half as much money and twice as much time* ought to be tattooed on the cerebellum of every parent.

In addition, make good rules and stick to them. Be what you want your teen to be because he or she is taking most of their clues from you. And love your kids for who they are, not because they make you look good or conform to some ideal, but because they're unique individuals. Make signs of that love clear and frequent.

Navigating choppy seas

Being half-child and half-adult, teenagers are navigating one of life's choppiest seas. As they pitch and roll in these huge waves, our kids desperately search for a lighthouse. And what are lighthouses? Fixed beacons of light that signal where the dangers lie. They're stable. Strong. Enduring. Illuminating.

Can you be a lighthouse for your teen?

Recommended Reading

Monica Ramirez Basco, *Never Good Enough: How to Use Perfectionism to Your Advantage Without Ruining Your Life* (Touchstone Books, 2000)

Robert Brooks and Sam Goldstein, *Raising Resilient Children* (Contemporary Books, 2001)

William J. Bennett, *The Book Of Virtues: A Treasury of Great Moral Stories* (Simon & Schuster, 1993)

Ross Campbell, *How To Really Love Your Teenager* (Victor Books/SP Publications, 1993)

Suellen Fried and Paula Fried, *Bullies & Victims: Helping Your Child Through the Schoolyard Battlefield* (M. Evans and Co., 1996)

Daniel Goleman, *Emotional Intelligence: Why It Can Matter More Than IQ* (Bantam Books, 1997)

Judith Rich Harris, *The Nurture Assumption* (Touchstone Books, 1999)

Be a Parent, Not a Pushover

David R. Marks, *Raising Stable Kids In An Unstable World* (Health Communications, 2002)

Matthew McKay, et al., *How To Communicate: The Ultimate Guide to Improving Your Personal and Professional Relationships* (MJF Books, 1997)

William Pollack, *Real Boys: Rescuing Our Sons from the Myths of Boyhood* (Owl Books, 1998)

Lynne Oxhorn-Ringwood and Louise Oxhorn, with Marjorie Vego Krausz, *Step Wives: 10 Steps to Help Ex-Wives and Stepmothers End the Struggle and Put the Kids First* (Simon & Schuster, 2002)

Helpful Web Sites

www.aacap.org
American Academy of Child & Adolescent Psychiatry
> *Click on "Facts for Families and Other Resources"*

www.helping.apa.org
American Psychological Association
> *Many helpful articles on family and relationships as well as information on how to find a therapist.*

www.aish.com/family

Aish HaTorah
> *This is a network of Jewish educational centers that produces much helpful information about families in general as well as Jewish families.*

www.medialit.org
Center for Media Literacy
> *Its programs include helping young people explore how media messages (print, verbal, visual, or multimedia) are constructed.*

Be a Parent, Not a Pushover

www.newdream.org
Center for a New American Dream
> *An organization that seeks to protect the environment by lessening commercialism; includes "Tips for Parenting in a Commercial Culture"*

www.focusas.com
Focus Adolescent Services
> *A vast and immensely helpful Internet clearinghouse of information and resources to support families with troubled and at-risk teens*

www.josephsoninstitute.org
Josephson Institute of Ethics
> *Includes "Report Card on the Ethics of American Youth"*

www.jumpstart.org
Jump$tart Coalition for Personal Financial Literacy
> *Promotes financial education for young people*

www.mediafamily.org
National Institute on Media and the Family
> *Provides parents with information about media products and their likely impact on children.*

Index

Index

Index

About the Author

Maryann Rosenthal, Ph.D., is a licensed clinical and forensic psychologist in private practice in San Diego. She is the mother of seven children and stepchildren. Dr. Rosenthal is trained as a mediator in the theory and practice of divorce and child custody and is a recognized authority on parenting. She often testifies as an expert witness in court hearings. Dr. Rosenthal was appointed by the Governor of California to advocate for the rights of developmentally disabled children, teens, and adults. A popular and dynamic speaker, she appears frequently on radio and television to speak on parenting, family dynamics, and life achievement issues. For more information see www.askdrmaryann.com.

Dale Fetherling, a former journalist, has written or co-authored a dozen non-fiction books.

Maryann Rosenthal

For more information about ADULT parenting
and Maryann Rosenthal, see *<www.askdrmaryann.com>*
or email *DrMA@askdrmaryann.com*

For single and bulk orders, please contact Midpoint
Trade Books, *<www.midpointtradebooks.com>*
or phone 800-742-6139